RIDER HAGGARD, HENRY MILLER, & I

# THE UNPUBLISHED WRITER

## Other Titles By J. Marvin Spiegelman, Ph.D.

*The Tree of Life—Paths in Jungian Individuation*

*Reich, Jung, Regardie & Me—The Unhealed Healer*

*Rider Haggard, Henry Miller & I—The Unpublished Writer*

*Jungian Analysts—Their Visions & Vulnerabilities*

*Jungian Psychology & the Passions of the Soul*

*The Nymphomaniac*

*The Quest*

*Psychotherapy as a Mutual Process*

*A Modern Jew in Search of a Soul* (with Abraham Jacobson)

*Sufism, Islam & Jungian Psychology* (with Pir Vilayat Khan)

*Hinduism & Jungian Psychology* (with Arwind Vasavada)

*Buddhism & Jungian Psychology* (with Mokusen Miyuki)

*Catholicism & Jungian Psychology* (editor)

*Protestantism & Jungian Psychology* (editor)

*Judaism & Jungian Psychology* (from University Press)

*Pyschology, Mysticism & Magic* (with Israel Regardie & Christopher Hyatt, Ph.D.)

And to get your free catalog of *all* of our titles, write to:
New Falcon Publications (Catalog Dept.)
1739 East Broadway Road, Suite 1-277
Tempe, Arizona 85282 U.S.A

RIDER HAGGARD, HENRY MILLER, & I

# THE UNPUBLISHED WRITER

J. Marvin Spiegelman, Ph.D.

NEW FALCON PUBLICATIONS
TEMPE, ARIZONA, U.S.A.

International Standard Book Number: 1-56184-033-5

Library of Congress Catalog Card Number: 94-66059


First Edition 1997

Cover art by S. Jason Black

The paper used in this publication meets the minimum requirements of the American National Standard for Permanence of Paper for Printed Library Materials Z39.48-1984




Address all inquiries to:
NEW FALCON PUBLICATIONS
1739 East Broadway Road Suite 1-277
Tempe, AZ 85282 U.S.A.
(or)
1209 South Casino Center
Las Vegas, NV 89104 U.S.A.

# TABLE OF CONTENTS

# INTRODUCTION

As the title suggests, this is a sad book. It is a record of the experiences and reflections of an unpublished writer — myself — as he finally finds a publisher for his work, but one who turns out to be incompetent or fraudulent or both. But this is also a funny book. It starts out being the adventure of the writer's encounter with a dead author, H. Rider Haggard, and an Angel, all of whom go to the Land of Tewfik wherein a Green Man and an Orange Lady hold sway. This has got to be funny, I think, at least in the sense of "peculiar," if not also "ha-ha." Furthermore, our unhappy, unpublished writer is welcomed there and honored very highly. Finally, this is something of a mysterious book, taking up issues of fantasy and reality, good and evil, spirit and matter, vanity and service, ego and Self.

As I look at the book now, some twenty years since I undertook the writing of it, I realize why I began this introduction as if I were writing about another person: it is both I and not-I. The "Unpublished Writer" that I was then has been superseded by one who has fifteen books to his credit and the sadness and defeat have given way, too, to a sense of joy and fulfillment. Perhaps present readers, especially other "unpublished writers," will take heart from this. That period, the early 1970's, was a time when I wrote *Reich, Jung, Regardie & Me: The Unhealed Healer,* (New Falcon Publications, 1993) a "true story," like that of the Writer, but including a relation with the fantasy world also. How could I not, as a Jungian, be deeply involved with the imagination? I also wrote about "The Empty Teacher" and "The Unfrocked Priest" at that time, fantasy figures but related to life experiences as well. This group of failures finally came together with the "Powerless Magician." Out of that came a book entitled *Failures and Successes,* which will also appear in due course.

Some people, particularly writers, might like to know how this all came about. In my teens, I had the writerly desire, as do

many, and fulfilled this by working on my junior and senior high
school newspapers and yearbooks, as well as writing stories.
During my years as a sailor in the Merchant Marine during
World War II, ages eighteen to twenty, I wrote a book about my
experiences. I hoped to get it published, finish college, and then
go back to sea, writing stories and shorter works, being able to
write a "deep" book at the age of forty. I thought I was a second
Jack London. When my book failed to get published, I turned to
another profession, ultimately becoming a psychologist and
Jungian analyst. I felt as passionate about this as I had been
about writing, and was surprised, when I turned forty, that I was
moved to write fiction again, calling it "psycho-mythology."

For several years I was deeply absorbed in this writing, which
made up for my loneliness when I felt the inner necessity to
resign from my local professional group and wrote three books. I
was pleased with the result and was gratified, too, when my
friend, the writer Henry Miller, also found it worthwhile. Even
Anais Nin, whom I knew only casually, supported my writing by
asking her publisher to consider the work. Despite this encouragement, I received some forty rejections from as many publishers, a numbing and ego-reducing experience, as most writers
know. At last, a small, local publisher was found, with whom I
was to publish the first one, *The Tree,* as a joint venture. At the
same time, I dreamed that H. Rider Haggard, a writer whose
work touched my imagination very much, came to me from the
dead, looking for a relationship. The present book begins at this
point.

What might it mean that an "unpublished writer" book needed
to get written and published? I think that it, like the "Unhealed
Healer" book, was necessary as an experience of failure, one that
many — if not most — people undergo at one time or another,
but few have the possibility of getting their experiences and feelings in print. I think that the very extensive suffering of that
period is redeemed by this fact: it serves as a statement for the
many who undergo it and few can express, thus also serving as a
possible solace (and even a source of merriment) for those who
endure such painful conditions. I hope so. In any case, it is to
those suffering writers, published and unpublished, that I dedicate this book. In particular, I want to pay tribute to my friend,
Helen Janiger, a writer who wrote voluminously but grew ill and

died before she could see her work in print (except for one small jewel of hers which is included in my book, *A Modern Jew in Search of a Soul,* co-authored with Abraham Jacobson). I wish that she, like H. Rider Haggard, could get some value out of continuing to be "known," if only in the psyche of another appreciative writer. All serious writers, living and dead, as Haggard said, serve the Muse in one form or another, since the psyche itself is eternal.

The early 1970's, my forty-fifth until my fiftieth year, were surely a period of "nigredo" for me, the darkness spoken of by alchemists and mystics. The subsequent "albedo" and "rubedo," whitening and reddening, also took place, I hasten to assure other frustrated writers, and my "harvest time" has grown in earnest since my middle fifties, expressing the many-colored "peacock's tail." Astrologers speak of the first twenty-eight years of life as times of growing up, taking up a profession, marrying and beginning a family. So it was for me. They also speak of the second twenty-eight as a time of enhancing one's being, fulfilling one's destiny, suffering one's Self, so to speak. So it was for me. The third twenty-eight, beginning at age 56, is the time of harvest, and so it seems for me, too. I am glad I could conform with that pattern, but I do wish I could have known about it in advance, as it would have softened the suffering! But that is the point, perhaps. If I had not had the suffering, I could not have written the present book and its sister. The reader will have to decide for himself/herself if it was worth it. In "serene" retrospect, I think so.

Next, I want to thank my good friend, Gilbert Phelps, Fellow of the Royal Society of Literature, for adding his support, as did Henry Miller, to this peculiar kind of literature. The encouragement by a "real" writer, like Phelps (I am just a psychologist who also writes), has been of inestimable value. In the many years that I have known him, I have been impressed with his own dauntless courage in the face of the vicissitudes and rejections that come to most writers, even one such as he who has enjoyed great literary success with both critics and the public. But that mutual experience of friendship in the midst of worldly rejection will, I hope, itself be part of another book, jointly written, to appear in the future.

Finally, I want to thank Christopher S. Hyatt, Ph.D. my publisher, for risking the publishing of my work when it had such a dismal previous record. That all my subsequent books have "panned out," to use the gold-miner's apt expression, is a fitting reward for us both.

J. Marvin Spiegelman
Studio City, California
Summer 1990

POSTSCRIPT

The foregoing introduction was written in the belief that this book would soon appear. As one might have expected, given the obstructive history, a significant delay transpired. It is now some six years later, a quarter of century since *The Unpublished Writer* was first begun. A couple of years ago, my dear friend Gilbert Phelps died, and we were not able to actualize the joint work that we had planned. He did, however, at my suggestion, write his "Confessions of a Failed Writer" before he died which I hope will be published one day. That an author such as he, who enjoyed both popular and critical success, could harbor such feelings might be consoling to the many writers who may be attracted to the theme of this book.

JMS, Fall 1996

# HAGGARD RENEWED

I am an old fan of H. Rider Haggard. There are, no doubt, many like me in their late forties and older who still are — even my uncle, God rest his soul, who just died at the age of seventy, loved *She* when he was a lad. Yes, everyone, that is everyone who reads (there are fewer and fewer readers these days), has known of "She Who Must Be Obeyed," and of *King Solomon's Mines,* even if only from the movies. So there is nothing especially significant about being a fan of the great writer.

But what is significant is that recently H. Rider came to visit me. One day, as I was thinking about my own writing and how thin it seemed these days, how little there was of true story-material in it and how panicky I was about it, there appeared the spirit of H. Rider Haggard. He not only said that I was a good writer, that I could have access to stories whenever I wished, but that he would see to it that a book of his that I had not read, *Wisdom's Daughter,* would come my way in due course. Then, he added nonchalantly, that I could write a story with him, a mutual creative work. Well, that was in line with many of my ideas, so I got excited.

I thought, "All right, I have been having difficulty with my writing and in getting published; how about working with someone as wonderful as H. Rider Haggard? So what if it isn't 'really' H. Rider Haggard, but a ghost, or a function of consciousness carried in my own psyche? Does it matter? Only to the individuality of Haggard, I would presume, and he is long dead. Let me go ahead and see what happens. If it works, fine. If not, well then; it would only mean another defeat in the long line that I have already had."

"All right then, H. Rider," I said. "Come along. Let us share this story that you have in mind. You start, and I will add my share as we move along." I see him, now: a handsome man, dark-haired, mustached, nicely dressed. He speaks:

"This story begins with a scene that you might recall from another of my tales, *Alan Quartermain.* It is a vision of a river surrounded on both sides by very high cliffs. I — that is, now, we — are moving down this river in a small boat which is steered by an oarsman who is with us, standing at the rear of the boat, taciturn. He is an African, tall, handsome. The three of us are silent as we progress down this river. Its character, however, is not so typical. On the one hand, it is in the African rain forest, but on the other, it is high above the world, as if in the air, with the water contained in a river bed which is open, below, to the empty sky. The cliffs above are supported by nothing but air. We steer through both domains simultaneously. And there are two sets of us, one set in each bark.

"We are in two stories, two dimensions. One in Heaven, you might say, one on Earth. Yet, of course, it is not Heaven as such, merely another dimension. We are substantially the same in both domains. Only our oarsman is slightly different. Below he is clearly African, above he is mercurial, vague."

Now, I, Marvin, ask, "Whither do we go and to what end?"

"Down the river of life," says Haggard, "and to the end of death."

Banal, think I, and wonder if this is not more illusion, until we come to a sharp turn in the river, almost man-made in character, and veer towards the right. As we continue, there is tremendously bright sunlight, in contrast to the gloom of semi-darkness of the lower dimension earlier and the sunset quality of the upper. Now both are in bright sunlight, almost blinding, but the two dimensions shift: two different events are happening.

In the upper dimension, we approach a throne which is bathed in intense light. Upon this throne sits an old figure, a man with a beard, as seen in the pictures of Zeus or some of Jehovah. To his right there is an angel, muscular, dark-haired, friendly, and gentle, known as Raphael. The bright light is focused on the throne and figure, but also billows out a little. The angel's wings seem more sculptured than real and he has no light around him.

In the lower dimension, there is no such throne or angel; there is only a sandy beach with pleasant trees. In the lower dimension, on earth, we beach our little boat and rest upon this beach under the trees.

Above, we approach the throne of this figure. We are not at all worried nor frightened, even if this is God Himself. Both of us have been used to dealing with images of God, of being beaten, deceived, enlightened, made ecstatic, experiencing joy and sorrow with such things, so we are merely anticipatory.

Several days have passed since I wrote the above. I have been both excited and fearful: excited by the prospect of really embarking upon a writing adventure with the great H. Rider Haggard; fearful in anticipation of the writing being poor, shallow, banal, just as I had said when Haggard described the river as the "River of Life." I have also had some thoughts about Haggard, which I have just checked. I had not known what the H. in H. Rider Haggard stood for. What came to me was "Henry". That proved to be correct, but would surely not in itself carry much weight as either a clairvoyant bit of information nor something from this personage to indicate that it was, indeed, *the* H. Rider Haggard after all. But what also came to me were dates for him: born in 1856 and died in 1938. When I looked it up, I found that his true dates were 1856 and 1925, so half right. Could, of course, be ... what do you call it when you have read something and don't remember it, and then come up with it? ... oh yes, cryptomnesia. Then again it could be "half" clairvoyant. But no matter, I am here to try and write a story with him, so let me get into the proper frame of mind.

"H. Rider Haggard, here I am, ready for us to continue the tale which we have begun. Are you there with me?"

"Indeed I am, Marvin, and you were half right in getting my dates. It was not cryptomnesia, it was the real thing. In time, I think that you will be more clairvoyant about me, but I do not wish to press that. I would much rather that we continue our story. Is that all right with you?"

"It certainly is. I think that we were standing before the throne of the great sun-figure above and quietly beached in a pleasant place below. Isn't that right?"

"Yes. There we are, standing before the great figure on the throne. Do you know who it is?"

"No, I do not. Father Time is what occurs to me, but I do not know if that is who it is."

The austere and radiant figure of the old man softens. A smile forms about his mouth as he strokes his beard and chin.

"I am not Father Time as you think;" he says, "nor am I God. But I do have much to do with time, and space as well. You two, in beginning your adventure, must first have conversation with me. I am, so to speak, a ruler of the Entryway. Your intentions, qualifications, gifts and such, must be assessed before you continue.

"I know this one, Mr. Haggard, but you, sir, are not known to me. What is your intention in beginning such an adventure? Do you realize that you are presuming, not only to having intercourse with the dead, which would make you something of a hero like Odysseus, but even to share a creative enterprise with them, making you more than a medium?"

"Yes, sir," I respond. "I realize that my desire is great, but it is not hubris which pushes me to do it, but a longing for greater creativity and, I must add, to deepen myself in the occult field."

"Are you sure that it is not merely the seeking of fame or personal power?"

"No, I am not sure of that. But my ... dare I say it ... my friend here, H. Rider Haggard, long since dead, seems to be willing, even eager, to share this adventure with me. I do not know his reasons, though."

"No matter; I know them, and that is sufficient. He truly seeks a creative work and therefore is advancing all our common aims."

"All right, but suppose I wanted fame and fortune. Are these bad desires to have in this enterprise?" I ask.

"No, they are not. I am merely asking you to be clear about it."

"Well, then, I am fairly clear. I do not seek fame and fortune alone, but I do not mind having them. It is creativity, the joy and pleasure of it, plus new knowledge that I seek."

"All right, then, you may proceed on your way."

"No tests? You have not asked my qualifications. I am something of a writer."

"Well, I presume that you are all right on those grounds, since Mr. Haggard would not pick just anyone. You may proceed. Furthermore, should you need my help, please call upon me, for I can shift my power and energy to this angel here and be of use to you. His stone-like, unliving character is only because he is not, at this moment, enlivened. I can, of course, shift myself to that vessel and form and be at your service. You see: one for judging (Father Time), and one for serving (the Angel)."

As he said these words, the old man smiled again. My thought was that he was easy enough and that one could learn from him too. He seems to be able to shift energy and forms rather easily, as well, or so he says. I look over to Haggard, or should I call him Rider ...?

"Call me what you wish, any of my names will do. Yes, I think that the old man is decent enough. And I am glad that we have made our peace with the gods above. Let us now return to our mortal forms — (forgive me for using that expression: it is an old one and I use it out of habit) — on earth."

We now find ourselves on the little beach below. I look at the oarsman and have the uncanny sense that this black fellow is, in reality, the same as the Father Time/Angel that we just met. My hunch is that he is the same mercurial figure that shifts forms all the time — accompanying, testing, showing, deceiving, aiding. But there is no clue from him about this. We are ready to continue with our adventure.

We are resting upon this sandy beach. I turn to Haggard, as if to ask, "What is next in our story?" He smiles, as if to say, "I thought you had the next idea." Now I smile and laugh because, of course, I don't. So we both turn to the oarsman. He says nothing, but looks up. I think that he is referring to the old man or angel, and I remember that the old man said that we could call him if we wished. All right then, I think that I shall summon him and ask his blessing.

No sooner is the wish felt than there is a vision of the old man and angel above. I watch as the old man starts to transfer his vitality to the figure of the angel. It is as if a substance and light are going out of him and flowing to the bodily form of the angel, whose body seems more fleshy or substantial than the light-body of the old man. Soon, only an outline of the old man is left, and then even that dissolves itself into a mere point. I understand that the point remains; should the old man wish to reconstitute himself in that form, the "makings" would be there. In the meantime, the angel has received the energy and vitality. He does not seem like a light figure, is rather more fleshy and earthy and available to us. I wonder about this transfer of energy and the changing of form: desire leads to change and production of the desired thing.

The angel sinks down and enters into the body of our oarsman. The earthing of our experience of the old man is complete. From a being of pure light, to angel (who mediates between the upper, heavenly realms, and the lower, earthly realms) to oarsman or guide, who can be with us in our full humanity. All right, that is how it is. But we are, after all, interested in our story and adventure, so we turn to the oarsman to be our guide. He is inspired with heavenly energy after all, and we hope he will direct us.

Haggard and I now follow the lead of the oarsman who motions us back into the boat. We continue down the river. As we glide along, we come, in short order, to a lion-like figure. But this lion is a strange one. He is both real and a drawing or picture of one. This is hard to describe, since the image changes from a black and white drawing to a real lion. I have to conclude that he, like the oarsman, has at least a dual nature.

The oarsman stops, throws out an anchor, and squats in the boat, looking at the lion and waiting. We do the same. The lion opens his mouth wide. We look inside and have a sense of wanting to go in there, but it seems questionable. If it is real, who wants to be devoured by a lion! If it is a mere "drawing" or image, then there is not much vitality or importance to it. So we are stymied.

"What do you think, Haggard?" I ask. He shrugs his shoulders. I am wondering why he came along in the first place. I had great admiration and hopes for and from him. Now he seems less heroic, adventuresome, wise, or even much of a writer! I would be tempted to conclude that this nit-wit is nothing else than my own "inner" writer! But I can see that there is no use in putting myself or Haggard down; something else is intended.

I begin to glimpse that there is already a lesson being shown here, perhaps a task of some nature. It dawns on me that what the old man-angel-oarsman has in mind is the problem of "reality." What is real? Is it the image? Is it the flesh? Yet all of this is an image going on in my mind. Or is it only my mind? Is it not also, possibly, really the ghost of H. Rider Haggard? I got one of his dates right, after all, and maybe he exists apart from my own fantasy as well. And now this lion and his reality are at issue. Yes, I can see that we are dealing here with image and energy, reality and fantasy. All right. I shall sit now, with Haggard and the oarsman, and stare into the lion's great mouth.

As I do, I feel pain in my belly: a kind of sickness. I think of my own greed, wanting to trust my own inner animal, yet finding it is not to be trusted, since it leads me into over-eating, over-drinking, and then requires "discipline." I look at Haggard. He seems trim and healthy, but so am I, actually. And the oarsman is the picture of strength and vitality. So then, what is this pain, and what is the next step with this lion?

I wait some more. Now I sense that the lion-image is fading. Its energy starts coming across the water to our bark. The oarsman has been concentrating upon it fiercely and intently. The energy of it seems to come across the water, as I said, towards Haggard and myself. The lion-animal part enters into Haggard as it approaches us, while the drawing-figure part comes into me. That has the effect of making Haggard more fleshy and "real." I can understand that: the ghost takes on more "reality" as it takes on flesh. But what does the drawing part or image do to me? It collapses upon itself into a point, just as the old man did, and lodges in my belly, near the navel, aligned with the solar plexus.

Ah, now I begin to understand once more. The lion is also like the sun in symbolism: he is identical, at an animal, instinctual level, with the old sun king. That he becomes internalized in me at my solar plexus seems quite right. So then, it would seem necessary that the energy-changer-transformer becomes a function of my own belly center and that the solar plexus, a place of power, carry its authority. Meanwhile, the ghostly writer, Haggard, takes on more "flesh" and becomes more "real."

But is this a story? Or merely another futile fantasy in which there is no real change? Merely another shift in the mercurial reality of the soul, which is all image and flow, no effect in flesh or spirit? Let me turn to the mercurial one, the oarsman-king-angel, and confront him with that.

"Oh King, changeable one, show me the reality, the vigor of truth! Where is the true creativity and flow of you?"

The oarsman merely blinks at me, like some iguana or member of the lizard family. No words come from him. I turn to Haggard. He too, says and does nothing. What am I to do?

I re-read what I have written and do not think it much of a story, nor even very interesting. More disappointment.

"O.K. for you, H. Rider Haggard! O.K. for you, King and oarsman, Mercurius and angel!" say I, like a six-year old. "O.K. for you! If there is no creativity in you for our work, then nothing happens and you are also stuck in unreality and boredom! How do you like that?"

This plea to these figures to manifest more, to come into my existence with greater power and creativity, seems not to effect them much. O.K. This is a story all the same. It is my story, at least, and story is what counts. Whether any one else thinks so or not, it counts. O.K.

"God! O.K. for You! If You are there. Or are You, too, a figment of my fantasy, without effective reality? Well, my old image of God may be that, no longer effective. O.K., you guys, it is up to you. Ball in your court!"

Another day has passed, and I am back here at my typewriter, wondering if Mr. H. Rider Haggard, Englishman, gentleman, writer, and now friend, has accepted the "ball being in his court." Will he help us on our way, in both story and learning? He has been enlivened, after all, with the energy of the lion, and I have taken in and grown firmer with the drawing thereof. That leads me to think that he has more animal reality than he did before and that I have more of the abstract reality of a writer than I had. I did, after all, affirm my "writerhood" at the end of our last encounter. So here we are: not square-one, as the English would say, but each of us has changed some. What, then, do I see?

Haggard smiles at me pleasantly and acknowledges that the ball is truly in his court. I wait expectantly for him to act or speak. He just smiles. Now his lips move noiselessly and he holds his stomach as if in pain. As I wonder what his pain is, there emerges from him, as if in birth, a smoky, ethereal substance. A sort of subtle body or ghost. It comes out of his navel, and he holds his round and bloated belly in his hands. The material comes out like the genie in the bottle, but it takes no form. It merely swirls about. Waiting for Haggard to take responsibility and action, I look at him. He now reaches for this etheric substance and starts to mold it. I wonder if he is going to form another Ayesha — another "She", another *anima* of his own being, like Adam with Eve. God did it for Adam, though, so it is not quite the same. But Haggard is forming no Eve and no "She". He is kneading and compressing this fine material as if he wishes to make it more solid, more concrete and less evanescent, less etheric. I watch.

As I look on, however, I begin to feel a pain in my own belly, quite concrete and burdensome. I wonder if this is mere gas pressure, maybe flatus. I remember the Master Psychologist saying somewhere that the spirit wind begins as a rumbling in the bowels; if it ascends to the head, it becomes inspiration, if it goes down, it becomes merely flatus. So then, is this what is happening? Am I waiting for the "inspiration" of the writer or the flatus of the fool?

As I wait, I have an image of breaking wind, though I do not do so concretely. Haggard laughs at me, but not unkindly. Rather, he has now made his etheric substance into a small figure, something like a little rag doll, but having the quality of a mannequin. He holds it next to his cheek, quite tenderly. I see that he is demonstrating the kind of attitude a writer ought to have in relation to his own creations and his own soul-body: tender, playful, like both a child and a god, creating a being. Yes, I think he is right. I have the image only of inspiration or flatus, above or below, and that is just another variation of "inflation," I suppose.

So, following Haggard's example, I concentrate once more upon the pain in my belly. First, I anticipate a child emerging or a woman, and then I glance up and see a picture of a phoenix rising from the ashes — the emblem of the publishing house. These images are too quick and mercurial, perhaps only anticipatory. Let me pause and wait a moment.

What emerges is a sequence of paper dolls. Back to the issue of paper; of real and unreal! "Balls!" I cry out, and Haggard laughs again. Now I see him juggling two balls, then three, quite well. I sit there merely holding my belly.

After this goes on for a bit, I pick up Haggard's little doll and hold it to my cheek. If I can't produce my own creations, at least I can comfort myself with his, I think. At that point, Haggard throws down his juggling balls and takes my hand. I feel his warmth and friendliness. I realize that this frustration was partly to make me more open to him, actually, and his creativity. Yes, this has really happened.

Haggard now begins to rise in the air, holding my hand, and I rise along with him, although I am very aware of the heaviness of my being and that my rising is far more difficult than his. He is, after all, a ghost from another dimension. He pulls me, all the same, and we are rising.

Soon we are above the clouds and see them below us, round, soft, a floor of marshmallow or cotton, with grayish parts too, like old snow on the side of a road. We also see the setting sun, which is very beautiful. Haggard looks at me and I know that he means, "Who can describe or write about such beauty? The writer's craft is not much compared to that. But that, too," he suggests as he points to his head, "is a creation of the mind, from the soul of the writer. That too." I am reminded of a book on the occult, suggesting that we all create our own reality, writer or not, artist or not. Our true being exists first in our psyche, our beliefs and our thoughts. How do we describe this to others? And where, please, is our story? I expected a writer to write and not be a teacher, did I not?

Haggard remains as he was, looking at the sunset with deep pleasure. As he looks, the whole sunset starts to compress into an etheric substance and to crawl into his head! Pretty soon, nothing is left except the emptiness of space. All is back inside Haggard's head. First he created his child-mannequin-doll out of his belly and now he takes in the vaster, impersonal God-creation of sunsets! Do I understand it? The writer takes in vast God-creations, transpersonal forms and images, and produces little creations out of his own belly and being. In that, he is a God-man, but not like Jesus Christ — a God-man who is a scapegoat, incurs suffering and undergoes self-sacrifice for mankind. A writer is a God-man in his imitation of God the creator, not God the self-sacrificer and healer.

O.K. As I said before, but no longer in an angry fashion, O.K. for You, God! It is indeed O.K. to be for God, therefore, in creation. Can I do this? Did Haggard do this? Maybe he did. I haven't read *Wisdom's Daughter* ... I just phoned the bookstore; *Wisdom's Daughter* is not in print, but *Erich Brighteyes* is, and I have ordered that.

"Well, Haggard, you will have to do something for me to get that *Wisdom's Daughter* now, won't you?" He nods.

We are still in the "learning situation" it seems, and not yet into a story. Not yet.

I feel the writer, H. Rider Haggard, there in the background, speaking softly. Thoughts come, such as, is he really there? Should I read more about him, be more in touch with his reality? A further thought: he died in 1925; maybe he re-incarnated as me in 1926! What a chutzpah, a hubris and an inflation! Yet, I recall, as a child, thinking that I was a writer in another life. I remember, at age 13 or so, when I tried the Rosicrucian experiment of being in a dark room and looking deeply into a mirror, with only one or two candles at the side; they said that previous incarnations would appear then. What appeared to me were two people successively: an old philosopher and a romantic young writer. I thought that I might have been Byron then, or Keats even. Later on, in the Merchant Marine, when I felt so at home in Denmark, I thought I might have been Kierkegaard! Well, now I understand that these were the archetypal forms of the young and romantic writer in me, as well as the dark, anxious, depressed but religious philosopher-wise man. But what about H. Rider? What about my search after REALITY? The truth of psyche and the spirit? What about all that?

"Are you there, Haggard? Are you there to accompany me, teach me, be an authority for me? My friend, the only one to have seen these pages, thinks that this is a great step. She thinks it is of first importance that I now am with an authority — a guide — and am writing more with the child in me: open, innocent, free, and child-like. What do you think?"

Haggard smiles pleasantly. He does not speak. Rather, he takes my hand warmly and shakes it, not in a greeting, but in a brotherly, affectionate way. He smiles once again and has me look into his eyes. I do. They are very brown, very dark. But I do not want to get lost in his soul depth; I want a relationship with him. Let me accept him as an authority and follow what he proposes. I look then into his eyes.

I see an ocean and on it a liner. This is a large steamship of the early years of the twentieth century. All these people are there, like the Titanic. But it is not that, I am given to know. I see Haggard on it. This is a voyage that he took to America, I think. He is trying to tell me something about himself in this way, in images. Yes, I see him, just as he looks now: handsome, slightly greying, mustached. He took a trip to America, he is trying to tell me. This is a "fact." That, he gives me to understand, is something that I can use to check on whether it is truly "he" or a "figment of imagination." Since I know practically nothing of his life, I could check on that. But now I remember that somebody in Zürich wrote about him and his work. There is information. Her book, I think, is in German however, and not likely to be available here. But, should I read about him? Or should I trust him to give me the information clairvoyantly? He said earlier that this would happen in due course. I shall await his decision on this. Right now, he shows me that he took a boat trip to America.

No, there is something further. He is interested in America, in what happens here. He is interested in the occult and that is why he is interested in me. I am trying to combine writing, fantasy, the occult, and that was unfinished business for him. No, I am not Haggard in re-incarnation, he seems to tell me; he has not yet chosen to re-incarnate at all. He will, in time, but just now he is quite busy trying to continue his work in combining art and the occult, just as I have been. That I also know the psychological aspect, well, so much the better, but that is of less interest to him. There are not too many who are in that field now, though there were several in his day, as I know too. There were Bulwer-Lytton and Yeats, for example, and later on, not known to him in life, Dion Fortune. He gives me to understand that there are, indeed, other writers interested in the occult. All right, Haggard, I hear you. But why do you not speak to me in words? You did before and you are, indeed, a writer and user of words, are you not?

You answer me telepathically, as if to say that words are not too trustworthy just now. Besides, you want my consciousness in this, too. All right, but what have I to offer? My ear, you answer, my devotion, my intelligence, and all the qualities that the old king wished to assess at the beginning. We had to pass his judgment, of course, before we could even really start our adventure together. Trust me, he seems to say. Trust me, Marvin. It is hard for you, who have been so often deceived and disillusioned. But try it once more. Have we not found that this is what the artist is? Open and trusting and creative like a child, and like a god?

Yes, Haggard. And, like God, suspicious and closed and destructive. Name your god and I'll name your attitude! But I shall not quibble, nor cavil, nor be destructive myself. Rather, I shall be open to you, to creation, to ... Where would you lead us now? Rest, you say. Leave off writing now and read and enjoy Haggard's own work. O.K.

... A day or so later. I had expressed the wish — or suggestion — as I went to sleep last night, that Haggard might come to me in a dream and speak of himself. If there was such a dream, I did not receive it. Are you there, Haggard? Are you there to go on with me?

I see him as before, handsome, quiet. He seems to return to the image that he gave me of the steamship of the early part of this century, the ship on which he came, I think, to America. What does he intend by returning me there? ... My thoughts go, too, to the cruise down the "River of Life" as he called it, and "to the End of Death," where we began. Then we had a small boat in the hinterlands of the African rain forest, yet also in the heavenly dimension. On that craft, Mercurius accompanies us. On this new great steamship, there is another kind of voyage. What is he saying? That there is an outer, concrete ship, with the H. Rider Haggard who once lived and wrote, and that there is an inner, occult, psycho-mystical Haggard, who accompanies me and is interested in a mutual search? Yes, that seems to be it ... But which way shall we go, Haggard? Shall it be to improve or try or "prove" (test) my occult powers of clairvoyance, or shall it be to continue our inner adventure? I leave it to you.

Haggard ponders over this. He takes off his suit jacket and white shirt and grabs an oar. We are once again on the small bark on the narrow river. But now Haggard rows and I am guiding and directing. Strange, a minute before I asked for his guidance, and now he is rowing and I am guiding! No matter, neither of us is really guiding, since it is a pair adventure and we must simply go down the river.

We go down once more, but now the Mercurius-black angel-guide is not with us. We seem to have left him back there, gazing at the lion. No matter, we know that he lives up in heaven and that he will appear in one of his many forms, should we merely request it. Enough, now, for us to proceed.

I watch Haggard row. He looks strong and flexible in the sunshine. I, too, want to row, so I summon Mercurius-black angel, take my shirt off and grab an oar myself. Now there is a threesome once again.

We row for some time, feeling the pleasure of the tug on our muscles, the stretching of our backs, the power of our arms. A good feeling accompanies us, while the steersman, Mercurius, quietly keeps our bark straight and sturdy. This is a calm river, the sides once again lined by sheer cliffs reaching high on both sides.

I have just re-read and edited the first part of my second unpublished book, "Son of the Knight," in *The Quest,* and I am moved by it. It is several years since I looked at it and I am pleased that it seems well-written, has a beautiful story. A good writer wrote there, better than the one who wrote the first one, *The Tree.* I hope and trust that this second tale will find its way into the world.

But what happened to that writer I thought myself to be? Here he is, most uncertain if he is a writer at all. What tale does he have to tell? What story of transformation, of adventure, of quest or myth? Seemingly none. Or not yet. It seems to hinge upon another writer, one long dead: H. Rider Haggard, famous writer and teller of tales.

Are you there, Sir Haggard? Are you there, Henry Rider? Are you there Henry Writer? ... You are. You nod, but you do not speak. Yet you assure me that all will be well. But now we are back on the river, rowing. We row in the sunlight while our oarsman, tall and black and quiet and royal, merely looks ahead, communing with the depths of his own innards, his own quietness. Down the River of Life, toward the End of Death, Haggard said. We row.

What, then, is this rowing, traveling, gliding, working, leading and be led, striving and being carried? Is not everyone on the River of Life, traveling toward the End of Death? Are we not all so led and leading, striving and being carried? And what am I seeking on this river, with this ghost and with this strange spirit? What do I yearn for, what do I seek? I, whose words are those of an unpublished writer, what am I doing on this river, with this ghost and spirit? Whom shall I ask this question, if not myself? And who shall answer, if not myself?

It is I, say I. It is I who am seeking on this river. It is I who wish to create, tell tales, flow like a river, yet swim into depths and eddies which astonish, delight, and inform. Writer would I be, who instructs with the touch of the tongue, yet feels the joy of the taught.

All this, friends. Like us all, I am rowing the River of Life, traveling with ghosts of the past, led by a spirit who is silent. But am I a writer? Do my words delight and inform? Not yet, say I, not yet. But my tale is of me all the same. No hero anymore, but yet my own. Are you there, Sir Henry?

"I am here. And why not? What else does a writer have to tell except the tale of himself? Even when he feigns and mythologizes. He reveals and conceals, informs and reforms, glides along the River of Life and tells what he sees. Does he see what all see? No. He sees drama, he makes drama, he reflects and pursues and, above all, he talks. His tongue becomes a wicked little worm, informed by fire, that teaches and deceives at the same time. Such is a writer. Should we tell this tale? Tell the tale of the failed writer? Is it a story? Yes, it is. River of Life to Death, Death to Life. Is there any other tale to tell?"

Haggard has now spoken, having been silent for a time. His words are true. I hear them, but still, there is the regular tale and the search. Now the quest is not for God, nor for Mother, nor for

Self, nor for Understanding of Love, as in my other books, but the quest is to write, to expression for itself, for the beauty and fire. The pleasure of it, the joy of it. That is how this writer needs to be transformed! Not only for understanding, not only for God, not only prestige-success-fame, but the sheer joy of it, as these cliffs are sheer. There is joy in the cliffs, here in the bright sun and the hard work, feeling the muscles of the writer rowing, gliding down the stream as the Spirit steers, flowing with the stream and telling thereof. All right. All write.

Now there is sadness, some days later, and I am not sure why. There is again delay in my book coming out. There is the irresponsibility of the publisher, nothing new, but also thoughts of how to write this book, "The Failed Writer."

"H. Rider Haggard, are you there? I bought some works of yours the other day, but could not find *Wisdom's Daughter*. Got *Erich Brighteyes* and some others, even read just a little about you — not enough to disturb the possible 'medium' effect we have going — but enough to get a feel for the man who wrote 100 novels, who was originally thought to be not bright, who traveled in Africa, was enormously successful as a writer. Doesn't matter, any of it, for our purposes, does it? Because we are doing a new thing. And even if your old style and verve and class are not in this writing, since it has to filter through my consciousness, still we are in it together. I know you loved the yarn or story as well as the occult — me, too. I hope I can be useful to you, too.

"I see you now, as before, looking at me, dressed in your nice English tweed suit, with your mustache and full hair. You smile. We are not rowing our boat down the river now. Is there a tale for us to tell? Something more than the story of the failed writer?

"You smile again and, in doing so, you cause me to smile, too. Why do you smile and why do I? Because it is funny to write a book about a failed writer. If the book is a success, then one is no longer a failed writer. If the book is a failure, then it is a true and boring picture. Well, that is not what I had in mind. What I had in mind was the transformation of the failed writer into the successful one! Well, we have been through that, haven't we? We decided that the work is the thing, the writing is the thing, successful or not. So, here we are, and I was — am — sad. Or am I, now? Not as much, having smiled. As William James said, perhaps I am no longer sad because I smiled!"

Haggard grasps my hand and holds it tightly. Suddenly, he closes his eyes, is very intense, and I share his vision of swirling desert sands. As the sand blows around us powerfully, I wonder if he is not getting us mixed up with T.E. Lawrence. Then I remember Quartermain and his trek across the desert in *King Solomon's Mines*. What a beautiful description! What imagery! One felt it so strongly in the reading. And I remember that he wrote this on a bet, as a youth, in just a few weeks! Well, Haggard, you are indeed a fine writer, and I salute you!

Haggard drops his head, rather diffidently, or is he embarrassed? But he raises it again and concentrates. Once again, he produces the swirling sand. I watch it as it gathers into a whirlwind and spins about his head like a turban. Finally, it congeals into a turban and I wonder if he is changing into a magician, but Haggard takes off the turban and opens it up. It is a small cornucopia, but only a little fruit comes out — an orange, a lemon, and a tangerine.

What is he trying to show me? Desert sand, created by him, whirled, forming into a turban which in turn produces a little fruit. I wonder what this means? Is it that the writer's powers of imagination cause and produce a whirlwind — a spiritual furor — in the dry sands of sadness and dryness (no water of life), and form it in such a way that it becomes a turban, a magical crown out of which a little fruit is produced? It does seem like that a bit. That is what is being done now. Out of my dryness and sadness, this whirling it about can create a magical crown, a storied vessel, which can produce fruit. But what is produced from this cornucopia? A few little items: an orange, a lemon, and a tangerine. Perhaps three little pages, sweet a little, bitter a little, and tart a little! Yes, quite, as Haggard would say.

"Well, Rider, my friend, you of many words; here you are, speaking nothing now for several meetings and producing images which I share. I play psychologist to your non-verbal play, but do we produce writing? Yes, they are words, but art? You shake your head no. They are life, you seem to say. This art is an art of life, like the treading and sailing down the river. Art is produced here, in life, a living story, a creative venture on the paper where two writers, one living, one dead, try to create a new world, where creativity and life, art and reality, become one. That is what you are trying to do, you seem to be saying to me, when I am just longing to write beautiful stories. You have a greater task, and I am your reluctant but equal partner, since my own words and consciousness have to be the vessel. All this you say to me, telepathically, and I get the point.

"Is there more? Do you have more to convey to me? Is it enough that there is, in fact, a little less than three pages of fruit in what we have produced: a little orangey sweetness, lemony bitterness, and tangerine tartness?"

I look to my friend and guide, partner and leader, and he merely smiles. This gentle Englishman, writer that he is, accepts that this, too, is writing, and part of our journey down the River of Life. Again I get a glimpse of us on that little boat, the intense light of the sun glinting on our oars as we glide and row. The steersman himself is now smiling and I see that it is he who now wears the turban of creation, the cornucopia of the fruit of imagination, and he smiles as we glide down the river. I feel the rowing, the pull of oars, stretching of muscles, the warmth of the sun. And I see my friend and colleague, Haggard, as we pull the oars together, firmly and easily, with faith and pleasure.

My friend has now also read these written words and asks: "Why does Sir H. Rider Haggard choose you to do a mutual creative work? I know you are talented and all of that, but if his task is the combining of art with the occult, he could choose any of the dead who were interested in that line, Dion Fortune, perhaps, or Crowley himself! Haggard could find these people and converse, work, play with them, could he not? Why does he choose a living mortal?"

As she put this question to me, I immediately thought of the traditional answer that it is just because I am mortal that Haggard has chosen me; the spirits want to work with the living after all. Did I not learn, long ago, that even God needs man to work out

His creation in the world? Even God needs a partner so that He can become conscious of Himself and even wants partners in co-creation. At last we finally find out that we are God, too! Yes, I learned this, with great cost and pain. But this, Sir Henry, is not the answer, I think, that you had. It did not seem right to me, since it was already known, nothing new. What is your answer? "I am mortal like yourself, J. Marvin. Just because I am dead and still speaking does not deny my mortality. I can, indeed, be born again, and the great God, of which we are all a part, will continue to grow and develop me, but this particular H. Rider Haggard has had his say in the flesh. Just because I have died does not limit my creativity, my possibility. It merely limits me in that I cannot be Sir Henry in the world again. Another form, yes, but not Sir H. Thus I am mortal, in the sense of limited. Secondly, my friend, it was not I who chose you, but you who chose me! Did you not know it? It was you who summoned me and I came. I came gladly, of course, and with my own aims, as I have described to you, but it was you who chose. Do you not know how you chose? Do you not remember? You did so many times. Remember when, as a lad, you read *She*? You were moved again and again. How frightened and angered you were by the savages! You were overwhelmed with She-Who-Must-Be-Obeyed! She transfixed you with her authority and her capacity to transform herself and live for so long. Her dance in the fire set your cells to tingling. It was not only *She* that made your being call out to me; it was also *King Solomon's Mines*. You knew the soul of these books, knew them deeply. The wandering in the desert, the search for the treasure of the past, and King Solomon, of course, all these you knew. You knew in wordless ways that were to become conscious and word-filled many years later. Indeed, that C.G. Jung also liked these books and spoke of *anima* and soul, of treasure and Self, all this rang true for you and it was this that helped you choose him, too! Did Jung choose you? Certainly not. He merely lived and expressed. Just as I did. But, of course, he also chose me! But he did not summon me. You, J. Marvin, caller of the soul, summoned me! You chose me and I came, obeying. Here I am. Or, should I say, as your countryman of old once said when his Lord called, "Here am I!"

"But I am not your God, Sir Henry! Unless of course, you are a mere figment of my own imagined creation."

"Yes, quite true. I am no figment and we are both engaged in creation. That, indeed, as I have said, permitted me to want to be called by you, chosen by you, be in a mutually creative work with you. Because of a need to combine the occult with art, creativity with life, just as I have said. It is here that we meet and in this work that we unite. But I did not summon you. You chose me!"

"These words ring true, Sir H. I chose you. I know what you mean. Yes, I remember all that you said. But I also remember sitting in my mother's mother's house one day, with the sun streaming in the window, and my uncle speaking of his own reading of *She*. How excited he was by the idea of re-incarnation! I was young and longed to be a writer. I knew that my uncle had once wanted to write but did not, and I felt a glow in that room, a strange feeling of presence. It was evening, and I felt something special. I knew that it was not something belonging to my grandmother or my uncle, or even, perhaps, to me, but I knew something was there."

"Yes, I was there, too, but you did not realize it. I was there then. For you summoned me. Your heart and your longing summoned me then, and I came. It was not *anima* that you sought, as Jung might have conjectured. It was I. And the Muse, of course. In that sense, Jung was right, too. The Muse is *anima* for a writer, but not quite in the same way that he thinks, or that you think either. But that remains for to speak about at a later time. It is enough that you know that you called me. You called me because the Muse had spoken with me and through me, in a way which resonated with you and with your feeling for the Muse. Not with my stories and not, of course, with my style, but with the Muse herself. And, summoning me, you called upon her, too. It is just here, with the Muse, that we must go forward, you and I. For the Muse is not *anima* alone, and she is not the memory of one's incarnations either. She is more — and less. And it is here that occult and art must come together more. It is hidden, even to me, and we — you and I — will go on and learn what and who this Muse is. She is more than *She* and more than … but, I speak too soon. There is much that we must do before we can pursue this question."

I pause here to take in what Sir Henry has said. It seems right
and I am excited and puzzled by his words about the Muse. Did I
say it right? Have I misused his spirit in the discussion of the
Muse? I realize that not every word that comes through will be
just his, filtered, as it is, through my own consciousness. And he
even disagrees with Jung! Imagine that! Well, I shall look forward to this work on the Muse idea. And I shall trust that he will
know the time. But now I need to recall another time when I felt
what he now calls his "presence": in reading *Alan Quartermain*.
Indeed, even the beginning of this work, sailing down the river
between the sheer cliffs, starts with that memory. He was there,
then. Those moments are of the Muse, he suggests. *Anima*, Jung
would say. Where the *anima* is, also said Jung, the Self is
present. And where the Self is, there is God too.

But I am forgetting where we are. The question is answered: I
have not been chosen by Haggard, I chose him. Why, I should
ask myself, did I choose him? Because he moved me so deeply
as a writer. He was not thought of as great — not a Shakespeare,
a Goethe, or even a Thomas Mann. I chose him, rather, because
his Muse spoke in a language that — dare I say it — my Muse
could resonate with. And now I hear that he needs me to help
advance his own understanding of the Muse. In this, there is a
combination of the occult and art. I remember now, my third
book, where I spoke to the Muses. It was a great experience and I
loved it. Now here is a chance to go on. Sir Haggard, I welcome
you and am glad that you came at my summons. We shall
proceed together ...

It is a day later, and I have gone through moods of despair and
joy. The despair came in the middle of the night. I awakened at
perhaps 4 o'clock, as I had wished, after reading in the occult
book (Seth) of the advantage of less sleep and being in better
touch with the unconscious thereby. Opening my eyes, I was
filled with frustration from not hearing from my publisher. His
endless delays and deceptions bring an agony of wondering
whether my book will ever come out. I questioned, *à la* Seth,
what am I contributing to having this frustrating, agonizing,
endlessly blocking experience of the failed writer, of the artist
who cannot get his work to appear in the world? Am I causing it?
If so, how? Or, if not me, then is the Self, as Jung described it,
doing it? This is the view that I have had in the past. The Self,

the greater totality located in me and around me and to be found in the face of every experience, is both encouraging me to write and blocking me from having the same words, this same vision, appear in the world. This paradox has been my understanding, and I have fervently, disciplinedly, honestly, devotedly examined myself, dialogued with my own inner Judge and also tried harder in the outer world. But still there is despair. Perhaps I should include herein all those notes to myself, all those statements written. Each of them is representative of a hundred others. These perhaps, should be included in this story of the failed, frustrated, feeble and fickle writer, but they are redundant, even boring.

In any case, after the darkness of the night's despair, came the morning of joy. Here was a different experience. I got up, did my daily exercises and stretches and joyfully went out for a morning swim. Because of an incipient cold, I had foregone this daily pleasure for some days — the first time I think, in months. I recalled also my daily half-mile noon-time swim at the YMCA and the pleasure of it. Today, however, there was a sweet outdoor smell, the trees newly fresh after a rain. A hint of buds was on the trees, even though this is only February. The sky was already clear, despite it being just after dawn, with a few clouds. Blessed Southern California after a rain. Blessed desert land when the smog is washed away. I felt renewed. The joy of this moment, the splendor of creation in nature swept around me and I felt glad. Our dog, Cleo, was delighted to see me swim again and she rushed around to find her ball and then to lick my hand at the end of every lap that I swam. And I felt fine indeed. There was no change in the facts of frustration. Doubts, fears that my book never would come out, all the anxiety that comes creeping in during the night remained, but another face of the Self was shown. It was the face of joy in life, in nature, in the beauty of the moment, experiencing one's body alive and moving, a vitality of being that continues right on through despair.

But, for the thousandth time, what is the meaning of this despair and frustration? Is it of my own making, out of an ancient sense that I am unworthy and thus creating this? Or is it from the Self teaching a lesson that I have not yet learned? Humility, maybe, or the joy of creation for itself?

At night I called out to God. I cuddled closely with my wife and longed for surcease from despair, the mind-bending question and the vise-tight restraints which kept me from even reaching that awful man, my publisher, a symbol of the tricky Mercurius. He is a wily, cheating, incompetent, sick, impotent being, who is both my vehicle to connect with the world from my own spirit, and the Satan-Hinderer who prevents it. Is all this the face of God? Or is it only the face of my own negative beliefs?

"Sir Henry, I beg you, speak to me of this condition. Tell me your opinion. I know that you did not experience such blockages in your life, having written and published a hundred novels and always, from the beginning almost, finding it easy to bring them out. But you are a writer, after all, and you know what it means to be published. You are dead as well and perhaps you possess some wisdom or perspective that I, in this mortal life, do not have. Seth spoke through Jane Roberts; what about you, can you speak to me about this?"

"Marvin," says Sir Henry, "I can not speak about you and your creativity-destructiveness. I do not know if the Self, as you call it, is performing this action of inhibition, or if you are doing it out of a sense of guilt or unworthiness. I have no access to such information and would doubt that anyone else would know this either. The dead are not, necessarily, more informed about the living than the living are themselves, unless the living believe it to be true. Here I am in accord with that occult man. But you could weigh these facts in a manner which would best accord with your own world-view. I can see that this world-view of yours is changing. I understand that you are coming to the perspective of the Creator God rather than the Suffering God. This I understand — from you. It does make sense. What I can offer you, however, out of my own existence as a writer is this:

"It makes no difference if it is you causing the obstruction, or it is the world that is doing it. It makes no difference at all! It is the obstruction itself that counts. As an artist, I know the pain of this. It is true that I was successful in life, in terms of books published and easy creativity. It is also true that I was pleased with my work. But do you know what success is? Most artists — and I have known many, living and dead, more I daresay than you — struggle always with the bitch success and what she means and wants. Is it success to be published? But what if you

are not read? And what if you are read, but not appreciated by
the critics? What then? Are you just a popular writer (a painful
term used of me in my lifetime, because the masses liked my
stories) and sneered at by the critics, the literati? Or, suppose that
you have a critical success — what is that French phrase, *succes
d'estime*, and sell a few hundred copies, but the people find you
boring, uninteresting, and you do not touch their souls at all?

"And further: what if you are both published and read, find
critical success, but you can not earn enough money to simply be
a writer? You must either find some other work to support your
art — which most painters have to do, after all — or live so
simply and cheaply that half the time you are as hungry for a
good meal or warm room as for fame and fortune.

"And still more: suppose you have all these, can they satisfy
you? Suppose that you are not really satisfied with your work.
And what artist is fully satisfied with his work, anyway? How
often can one look back on any particular piece, painting or
story, song or play, and feel quite satisfied? There is usually a
tinge, a criticism in oneself, a sense that one can/should do better. The inner critic is always worse than any outer critic. Hence
we can both laugh at the critics and dread them. It is just because
they portray the hardest part of ourselves. So then, which one is
success? Suppose, furthermore, that you are a happy man, successful, and like your work? But then, maybe you dry up, fall
into a vicious round of superficiality, of repeating yourself.
Marvin, I regret to say that this last is what I felt many a time.
Repeat and repeat. What new have you to say, Haggard, my
inner critic would question? I would cringe, but repeat, hoping
for the new. Sometimes it would happen, sometimes not. But no
matter. Each writer has his own wrestle with 'success' inner and
outer. As far as I know, it never seems to end. Now it is the lack
of outer success and no publisher, later it may be shallow fame.
Do you see?"

"Yes, Sir Henry, I see. It is dismal, I fear. I think that I would
be satisfied if my little book-children were fitted out with clothes
of paper and a cover and could walk around in the world on their
own. I do not think that I would be too greedy about it. I would
like fame and fortune, of course. That I acknowledged to the
Old-Man Keeper of the Gate at the outset, but I am not dependent upon it. I need my spirit out and accepted. I need to be

acknowledged as a writer. You know, as a child I wanted to be a writer. My aunt took my first book in dictation when I was six, and I always dreamt of being a writer. I wanted it right up until I wrote my first big book from 18 to 20, all about my adventures in the war. But my book was not published and I had to give up my dream, because I had to make a living somehow.

"My vision shifted to the study of the soul. It was a good decision and I do not regret it. I even fulfilled my expectation, at age 20, that I would only be able to write deep books when I was 40. So I did. But they are having a terrible time coming out into the world.

"Imagine! Forty queries to publishers, forty rejections! Many would have given up earlier. Even my writer friend, Henry Miller, is astounded at that. Imagine, too, all that I have had to go through with the publisher who is now supposed to be bringing my book into this world: delays, lies, broken promises, deceptions, barriers of frustration because of people's failings and needs, their inability to fulfill commitments and requiring so much care themselves. The business world seems very unbusinesslike to me. People need all kinds of attention, yet seem to exploit others when they can. Yet, through all of this, Sir Henry, I can see that I, unlike other writers, can make my livelihood in other ways, and so am not dependent upon the money from publishing. It would be nice, though, to have at least dual dependencies. One is not so vulnerable then in either place ... Anyway, you can see that success means something a little different to me. To me, with my history of rejection of my spirit from the age of 40 onwards, from others and from myself, success means that recognition, no more, no less."

"Maybe, Marvin. We shall see. For you shall surely be successful in those terms. But there is more to this than the success that you or I have spoken of. She, Success, is called Bitch-Goddess after all, and that she is. It is this that makes me want to pursue the Muse. Why is she Inspirer and also Bitch-Goddess? Do you know? For you that might be a psychological question and I have no quarrel with that. But for me it is an occult question and an artistic question. Who is this Goddess, really, who inspires us, wants us to speak? Who is she who also withholds from us, who also leads us into desires for fame and fortune? She is the same, I know. And so contradictory. But why? Why is the flaming fire of the soul so beautiful in fantasy and so ugly and painful when she meets the material world? Can you see, Marvin? Once again it is a question of art and the occult: art as the expression of the poetry of the soul and its images; the occult in its relation to the concreteness of matter, of the two-sidedness of art and material life. But here I, too, am confused. Here too I wish to know more about the Muse and what she wants of us. I spent my life in service of her. I wrote endlessly, but I know no more now than I did then. I too, want to know."

"Then perhaps we should consult her directly on these questions. I find you a bit vague in this area," I commented.

"Yes," said Haggard, "I acknowledge that I am vague, but I'm not ready to consult her directly. It is like taking on 'She Who Must Be Obeyed'! We shall both know when we are ready, don't you think? It needs time."

"Yes, I agree. And I am thankful to you, Sir Henry, for addressing my despair and my hunger. Your words do drop a seed into the damp earth of my emotions and I am sure growth will take place. I hope flowers, not weeds, will result!"

"All right, Marvin. No matter. 'Do what thou wilt' said Crowley, and I agree."

… More days have passed. I think it will be so long before my books are out in the world.

"Not so long," says Haggard. "Not so long. You have waited long already. Before you know it, the books will be coming out. One year, two years, three — a short time. Time perhaps, for us to find and pursue the Muse, the great Goddess, in a new way. Time to find her and learn afresh. Yet time is not and we are not — yet we are … I know your work with the Muse. That, too, is why I felt a kinship with you. We shall seek her soon. But rest now, my friend and weep for the failure. There too, is the Muse. She has a hand in it all. But you knew that. If one could only remember all that one has known! So much of existence is merely re-learning to re-member, to put together the sundered parts."

"I know, Haggard. But ... words ... feelings ... Better to row
with you on the stream, the clear river. I see it again. Aft is our
steersman, dark and taciturn as before. And here we are, rowing
and rowing. No words."

... Many more days have passed, filled with pleasure and joy
followed by frustration and despair at receiving no word from
the publisher. I finally caught him in his lair. I had previously
spoken to the printer, who brought me up to date: Yes, the book
had been "folded," and yes, at last it had been sent to the
bindery; but no, it was not yet being bound because the publisher
did not have the money to pay for the binding; well, he was
trying to get the money now; yes, many were in line with me to
get at him, creditors especially. Well, I went next door and luckily a magazine person was there to interview him about the use
of space. The door was locked, but I came in through the back
and startled the poor man. His "hello" was a bit strained, but he
took me into the other room and acknowledged where things
were, just as the printer said. He also passed on some rapid
words about somebody who was to have advanced him money
having died, and about another book having not worked out,
costing him $4,000; but I hardly listened to that. He assured me
that he would be getting the money, about $1,000, this week.
And yes, the book club was definitely interested. As soon as he
got an order from them, he could use that to print ... etc., etc.

I could only repeat, as I had before, that I was very frustrated
that he failed to answer my calls, to keep me informed at all. I
understood his financial struggle, I only wanted him to be honest
and let me know the truth. Would he call me on Friday, just to
keep me posted where everything was at? Would he do that?
Yes, he said, he would.

He gave me an unbound copy of the book. There it was,
beautiful, just like a real book. I was quite moved to hold it in
my hand, Sir Henry! Some tears came when I was back in my
car, gazing at the unbound book. The radio began to play Reverie
by Debussy, some love-music I enjoyed in my adolescence. I
said a silent prayer to God, of thanksgiving, sensing that grinding

pain and slowness would be overcome. I did not know if this was necessary or meaningful, but I surely would not experience the humiliating devastation of the book not appearing at all. I was at peace. What do you think, Haggard?

"I think it fine, Marvin. There is such a sweet joy for the writer, to see his words in print. A proper book, well! One has read so many books in one's life; one has admired, appreciated, been so impressed by books, that to see one's own — particularly one's first — that is truly overwhelming. I recall my own first book and the joy I felt in it — unforgettable!"

"What was that first book, Sir H?" I ask with trepidation, thinking that, for better or worse, I was testing the "reality" of this figure as Haggard or "figment."

"The book was *She!*, of course, the one that was to launch me on my career. I wrote it quickly and easily. I was in my early twenties as I recall, but She was clearly working inside me since I was 16. Just as the 'She' upon which she was based, the veritable Muse, was working upon you from the age of 16 onwards. Was it not my book and Hudson's book, Green Mansions, and Galsworthy's stories in the Apple Tree, as well as 'Irene', that sent you spinning and awakened that Muse sense in you? Even your wife bears the heroine's name in Green Mansions. You are a Muse-touched man if I ever knew one! Go ahead, check and see if *She* was not my first book."

"Haggard, I am chagrined and sorry to inform you," I said, "that I have just looked over the introductory notes in the New-castle Edition of your book, *The Saga of Erich Brighteyes,* and the editor there states that your first book was the semi-autobiographical, *Dawn,* published in 1884, when you were 28, and was followed in the same year by *The Witch's Head.* You wrote *King Solomon's Mines* in only six weeks in 1885, and only came out with *She* the next year, also taking six weeks with it. So you were about 30 when it appeared, and it was your third book!"

"So say the records, Marvin, but it is not true. I was already writing *She* when I was in Africa! As I said to you, the Muse — and 'She' — appeared to me when I was 16, and continued to haunt me, particularly during my days in Africa. The book itself did not appear until much later, it is true, but I wrote earlier drafts of it and was inspired by it all the time. It is not for nothing that it is thought of as my best book. It is, in truth, almost my only book. Believe me!"

"I am tempted to believe you, Haggard. It would be very convenient and would encourage me to go on with this project. If I did not, I should be in further despair. Not only a failed writer, in terms of publishing, would I be, but also a failed writer even in terms of his ambitious, interesting and meaningful project with a dead author! All illusion, then!"

"You see, Spiegelman, did I not tell you that? The writer meets with illusion, rebuff, dashed hopes, every step of the way. 'Success,' Bitch-Goddess that She is, is so easily lost. Yesterday you had a moment of joy and fulfillment, seeing your words in print. Even when it was not a proper book. It meant so much to you. And today you are in doubt whether it is really Haggard here or a mere figment. Your writing and hopes of 'success' can be totally crushed. It is so and will continue to be so. Ask any other writer if this is not true.

"But have no fear or further despair, Marvin. What I say to you is fully correct. Not only does the idea of *She* go back to the age of 16, but I was really writing it in my early twenties. Believe me. There is no way to prove this, I know. Nor is it terribly important, I think. It would be valuable, I know, to someone who is trying to prove the existence of spiritualism, but even though I am interested in art and the occult, it is not such 'proof' that interests me. That is more a concern of mortals, of course, who have no assurance of their own immortality, but not of us, the dead. Our — or better, my — interest in the occult is not of that sort. We, Marvin, are doing it right now. We are searching and trying to communicate with each other. Can you not see that this is truly occult? Can you not see that this attempt of the living and the dead, spirit and flesh, to cooperate and create something new is more important and occult than any supposed proofs? Who will listen to proofs? Only those who are doubting and want to be convinced. What is really convincing is one's own experience, to know deeply the link between the spirit and earth-realms. That is never given to one by means of external proof ... But you know this, I think, Marvin. Anyway, what I have said to you is true."

"Haggard, yes, you are right ... kind of. But I also want to find some of these 'proofs.' They would, after all, help my own conviction, I am sure. I realize that most others would not be convinced by such proofs, but some doubting ones might be. I guess I myself am such a one."

"Well, no matter, Marvin, if you need this, then you shall have this one day. Whether a proof emerges of the facts that I have mentioned to you or not is of secondary importance. No doubt such a proof will appear if you really need it."

"Yes. But there is disappointment in me, all the same, Rider. I grow sleepy or want to look again at the unbound copy. As if I want, once more, to reassure myself that what my soul produces has an existence, is not mere illusion ..."

"I understand, Marvin. Rest and read; refresh yourself, and then we will proceed to ..."

I return an hour later. I have napped, looked at the unbound copy and am ready to resume.

"Marvin, I wish that you would take up the dream that you had the other day," says Sir Haggard.

"Do you mean that involving the Tewfik people?" I ask.

"Yes, I do. I think you face a dilemma there similar to the one that you have with me. Do you not?"

"Well, yes, perhaps I do. As you may know, I had gone to bed asking God to send me a helpful dream. Instead, I awakened early, with a very dark and heavy feeling. I fell asleep once again, aware of the pain of my lack of recognition in the world, as I had desired it. It seemed that my book would never come out, that I would never be able to be recognized as a writer. And then I dreamed:

> I dreamed that I was being honored by the Tewfik people, for all the help and service that I had given them. These Tewfiks were a northern people, somewhat like Laplanders or Eskimo, but living a quiet, isolated existence, far from the rest of civilization. I was aware that their clothing was of a very intense green color and seemed to give off vibrations which were stronger than an ordinary green. I was pleased to be with them, impressed with their green, but puzzled by what it was exactly that led them to honor me.

"Yes, that is the dream," says Sir Henry. "Is that not a similar, dilemma-inducing situation? There you have a whole people, even named the Tewfik, who are said to be a living people, like the Lapps or Eskimo, but they are not a nation with which you are familiar. You could look into some geography or linguistic book, to see if such a people exist, but suppose they were not listed? Could these people not exist in another dimension, just as real as Lapps or Eskimo (whom you have also not seen, except in pictures and images, just as in your dream) exist in your reality? Could not the Tewfik live in space-time with their own reality?"

"I suppose so," I answer. "But then I could not ascertain if I were dealing with fantasy or reality. You, Sir Henry, claim at least to have lived a concrete life and your name and actual existence are registered in many books."

"Which, after all, is the only true reality!" says Haggard, with a laugh. "We both know that your need of having your book out is equivalent to the proof of your existence!"

"*Touché*, Haggard," I respond, "but that, of course, is of an order different from either a fantasy Tewfik and a Tewfik who have a registered existence in the material world. I do not challenge your assertion that there is a world — or even many worlds — different from the material one. I know only too well that the world of fantasy carries a force of psychological reality more potent than many a physical force. I know also that the myth, a fantasy reality, is truly what governs the nation, the tribe, and the person. And that it is this myth, particularly when unconscious, that determines existence, its form and direction. I know all that. Yet there is a difference in the two types of Tewfik and it is precisely this difference and the relation between them that poses the occult problem. Does it not?"

"It does, Marvin, and I agree. But the Tewfik may have lived earlier and been wiped out. Are there not stories of Atlantis, Lemuria, and other civilizations for which there is little or no material proof? Can there not have been even others, fully unknown and unregistered in the history books?"

"Yes, that is certainly possible."

"Well then, Marvin, what will you do about these Tewfik? Shall you just ignore them, interpret them as some dream manipulation, say something like it being a short-hand form of 'too fickle'? That would make some sense, of course, since recognition and appreciation from any people is far 'too fickle' indeed, for the artist's purpose!"

"Haggard, I do not know. I am certainly willing to 'dream on the dream,' as Jung used to say. I am prepared to continue the relation with these Tewfik people, if they are so inclined, and to find out more about them. In so doing, I would be learning more about my own myth to be sure. But would I be dealing with an occult reality?"

"It is just in this, Marvin, that I am interested. I am no more learned nor skilled in this area than you are. Just because I am dead does not give me that total information. I can assure you that death does not give one omniscience any more than one had in life. It is still a question of learning and experiencing. One learns only that material reality is far from the only one. But you, Marvin, already know that now, alive, while you are fully in the grip of mortal flesh."

"True, Haggard, and I grow confused. I can hardly keep up with the dilemma. I don't know which is which. That has happened to me before. As soon as I get deeply into the issue of spirit-flesh, matter and soul, I become confused or sleepy. It is as if, perhaps, the Witch does not wish me to penetrate this realm. Or, if I am allowed to penetrate, it is not with my full consciousness."

"Exactly, Marvin, exactly! Now you are approaching my dilemma as well. What you call the Witch is yet another form of the Muse. It is this quality of hers that be-deviled me — if you will permit a switching and mixing of metaphors — when I was alive. Precisely this unconsciousness and confusion blocked my own further development in that area."

"What then shall we do, Rider?"

"Well, ultimately, we shall have to see, take on and confront the Muse herself. But, just now I suggest we ..."

"Wait, Haggard! I just looked up and saw a spider crawling upon the wall. It was a little black one. You see, that old friend of the Witch and her web are present synchronistically! I also saw a little ant, a friend of work and order. These little creatures do not usually manifest in my work-room-study. These I take as the kind of occult event that Jung talked about, synchronicity: the meaningful coincidence of events in simultaneous but acausal and psychic reality ... Funny, the spider stays very still beneath an ancient picture of Jerusalem, the Holy City. It sits there, no movement. The ant has disappeared under the desk."

"I wonder what the spider wants," says Haggard.

"I would guess ... as soon as I said these words, the spider climbed up several inches and down again ... Now the ant reappears ... no, it is another spider. It climbs up an old manuscript of mine. I wonder what the Witch wants."

"Marvin, you again come close to my question!"

"It is a question that I think we cannot answer yet, Sir Henry. But we could visit the Tewfik people."

"Yes, let us do that," says Haggard. "But I sense your same uncertainty as with the issue of when I wrote *She.* Look up the Tewfik. I notice that the spiders have disappeared immediately as you were doubtful. Is that not so?"

"Yes. But I shall respect my doubts all the same and try to look up these green and not-so-famous Tewfik.

"... I have done so and have not found them. I have looked in anthropology books, folklore books, and even in Hastings' *Encyclopedia of Religion and Ethics,* but nothing. So, they probably have no historical existence."

"Again, Marvin, you jump to conclusions. Perhaps we should speak to the Tewfik before making pronouncements."

"All right, Haggard, I agree. If I asked God for a helpful dream and He sent one, the least I could do would be to continue the contact with the people He mentioned."

"Agreed. Our next meeting will pursue it."

... "It is a day later, and I am back with you, Sir Henry, ready to embark upon our joint task, but I am full of what has happened in relation to the Witch since I last spoke with you. I feel a certain inability, though, to convey the details of what has happened. It is as if the Witch herself is there to knock out my consciousness of things, particularly in the area of my own inferiorities, such as the awareness of and description of details (sensation) of events and the capacity to formulate from these details (extraverted thinking). My intuition, my feeling, and my introverted thinking capacity do not leave, but my other functions are merely gone. Further, I do not even feel the importance of dwelling on all the 'facts.' That, of course, further depotentiates me. I want to rush directly to the intuitive thought and image and work with that. Quickly to the archetypes, boys! Old Marvin is here to give the God's-eye view of the whole thing! No matter that he is stuck in old complexes. No matter that he gets hurt all the time. No matter that he stays split and/or the victim. He must be the savior-prophet.

"Well, I want out of that now, but how? Should I try and recount all these details, Sir Henry? Is that writing? Or art? Or even, can I do it? What do you think?"

"Why do you ask me, Marvin? I do not mean to be responding to a question with a question, as do your people, but can you see that your asking my view keeps you dependent, rather than working towards the consciousness you admired a moment ago?"

"You were there, it seems, Haggard. You heard what transpired between that person and myself?"

"I did hear and I was there. So, if you start to sort out what happened, you will do this for yourself."

"But, Sir Henry, is this writing? It seems only like more inner work, not writing meant for a wider public."

"If you think it is not writing, then it is not. Is not the Witch specifically a curser? Does she not, by making the statement produce the event? Is that not the same as the Judge, condemning?"

"Yes, I think you are right. But we are already into the 'fundamental image' and conclusion almost rather than following the step-by-step method."

"Yes, I think that is true, Marvin. We must acknowledge that the Witch — the other face of the Muse — is with us at every step and that we have to acknowledge her, both bow to her and fight her, do whatever seems necessary at the moment. Just now it seems necessary to describe some of the events that led to where you are right now."

"Yes ... my thoughts go back to the spider and the ant of yesterday. I think immediately of the Witch and of the Devil: Witch, from the web and the confusion of the spider, and Devil, from the limited and driven orderliness which can be seen in the anthill. But again I leap to images, to intuitive concepts! Slow, Marvin, slow, I tell myself.

"My thoughts go next to the witch-like contact with our dog yesterday. She had chewed the plants again, which made me so angry that I rejected her, drove her away. But her cringing, then coming to lick me, made me feel guilty and aware that I was too harsh. A dog, after all, has to chew! It is her nature. What is a plant and my will compared to her nature and being? So I forgave and petted her and felt better. But, still, I am angry and feeling myself a victim.

"Now my thoughts go to the conversation with L. about the Witch, in terms of mother complexes. There I saw that witch-like rigidity, cutting off of emotional exchange or connection, arising out of anxiety. We spoke of negative mother experiences. But how should one deal with that?"

It is days later.

"Now, Sir Henry, I am ready to visit the Tewfik, the green-clothed ones who live in a land that may not exist, but is a nation which recognizes and appreciates me when the world does not and I do not! So, Haggard, let us go to the Land of the Tewfik!

"But before we go, I want you to know about my twelve year-old daughter's dream the other night. She dreamt that I was awarded the Nobel Prize for Literature! What love, what appreciation! My daughter's love shines through. Her recognition is there. Maybe even the psyche is saying something through her. Somewhere in the land of my daughter's young psyche and in the bigger psyche, too, I am a good writer. Somewhere, too, in the land of the Tewfik I am recognized and appreciated. And so, Haggard, and so, Steersman, off we go to the Tewfik! Let us leave this African place of warmth and the swamp of my problems. Let us leave also this place of high stone cliffs and barriers. Let us take our bark to the north, to the Northern land of Tewfik. Let us leave Africa now and find that place that exists in some region where recognition lives, where value is received, where fantasy Nobel Prizes are won. Tewfiks are not likely to be Swedes, but maybe their land is next door!"

Steersman, Haggard, and I are leaving the river between the walls of granite. We enter the open sea. We paddle and steer our little boat up north toward the Land of the Tewfik. We cross the seas. We are real and of quite human size, but we also sail on a large map of the world, which is only somewhat larger than we are. That is to say, it takes us not long at all to get from here to there, from African cliffs and river to Tewfik ice and water. There, just above and beyond the lands of the Vikings, the land of Swede, Finn, Norwegian, and Dane, we come to Tewfik Land.

But Tewfik Land is at a point. It lies at the North Pole. Once again it is a point, as in the beginning, when we met the Keeper of the Gate, the God of the Throne of Judgment. Now the point is not a being or a god, it is a place and a state. It is a place, Tewfik Land, and a State, the state of Being Tewfik. We descend into that world, know that it exists and is real, yet is a point at which the worlds meet. These are called power points. They exist all over the world, such as at Stonehenge, the Pyramids, and Jerusalem. But here the point is the Pole itself. To reach Tewfik Land, one goes to the Point, but the Land is in the next region, the next state, the next dimension. It is a land of the future and the past; but most of all, it is a land of Being. It is a land of Green. All this comes to me before we even land, before we even see the place. Now I am to wait. Before entering Tewfik, I am to wait for another day.

"But Haggard," I exclaim, "We are there! We are at the entrance, you, the Steersman, and I. We are there."

"H. Rider Haggard," I announce, several days later, "I am ready to resume our adventure in Tewfik Land, if that is all right with you and our steersman. I have some trepidation about continuing and ... trusting ... The very word that came out in my teaching class the other day.

"That digresses me — to make transitive an intransitive verb. Trusting is the thing I do not do with the gods of this world. I have trusted the God within, but the God 'among' and 'outside' — well, he is truly a Saturn to me, blocking and hindering, demanding and restricting. But God is One, I have believed, and the Hinderer is surely part of that same God; that too, have I believed. What do you think, Sir Henry?"

"What do I think? I do not know. I experience God much as you do, Marvin: a living presence, here, there, and everywhere; as an active reality, being and becoming; as a quality to be related to; in short, as the Muse herself. For me, God is in the Muse; so that when you speak of God as She, I have no difficulty with that."

"How is it, Sir Henry, that you seem to know all my thoughts? If it is, indeed, you as a separate entity and being, the Sir H. Rider Haggard who lived from 1856 to 1925, then how is it that you know my thoughts, as if you were only a part of myself?"

"A good question, Marvin, and one that I would like to answer. My reply is simple. I know what goes on inside your head and heart because you allow it. You have opened yourself to my being, to my consciousness. You have withheld nothing from me. You did this when we first met, an act of surrender. You did it partly when you first read my work at 16 and then more consciously recently, when we began to write together. This was not a conscious decision on your part, as if to say, I now open my entire psyche to Sir H. Rider Haggard. Not that. Rather, you made a prayerful and trusting assent to what enters the soul. You are, I think, quite trusting indeed. You trust the world of the soul, as every writer must. That you do not trust the world of the flesh nor the world of organizations and nations and societies, well, I understand that. For there, of course, is where you have been injured, deceived, and defeated. The world of the soul, with all its dryness, its demands, its variety and swamp-like character, all that you have trusted. Else, how could you be a writer? So, you have trusted it ... and me. I am, therefore, able to traverse all areas of your psyche, as you call it, as I wish. Indeed, I think I find parts of your soul sometimes that you do not know about! But that is strictly because you allow it. At any time, you may revoke this privilege. Our connection is telepathic, but here in this act, in this joint effort, we are doing our real work: the work of the living and the dead, the quick and the unquick, the occult pursuit of life and art; in the writing, we are creating. That is enough. Your trust and, I might add, mine as well produce these words and pages, these thoughts, this dialogue, this art. Enough, don't you think?"

"I do, Sir Henry, I do … Let us, then, continue our adventure in the Land of the Tewfik."

We are at the Point: Sir Henry, the dark Steersman, and myself, and we dissolve into it, boat and all. We emerge at the place of the North Pole where the Tewfik live. But this, like our initial trip, when we met the Judge and also were rowing on the river, seems to be two realities at once. Tewfik Land is both a truly Northern one that is utterly snowbound and cold, but it is also green and beautiful, looking like an English countryside of Haggard's time.

"Indeed it does," says Sir Henry.

"I wonder why there are two realities again," say I.

"I can't imagine," says Sir Henry.

But the Steersman nods his head, as if he knows. He says nothing. We start to walk on the hills of the countryside and look for the green-clothed people who appeared in my dream.

I see them at odd moments, but I am not sure if it is truly they. What I see are little elves, dressed in green and scampering about, appearing and then quickly vanishing behind trees, shrubs, flowers, or disappearing under the ground. They tend to be tiny, no more than two feet high. These are not like the Tewfik which appeared in my dream. The latter were the size of human beings, were blond, and their green clothes gave off a radiance and intensity which was richer by far than that of these elves. The elves dart about us, grow more and more bold. They dash between our legs and dart away.

I pick one up, a very little one, and hold him in my hand. He is, truly, just like the elfin pictures one has seen, wearing a little cap with a bell, hooked nose, like a fool or jester, but in miniature. He speaks in a deep voice:

"Welcome to the Land of the Tewfik! We are not the Tewfik themselves, as you surmised correctly, but we are their helpers. Without our help, I daresay, they would not be the gifted, loving, marvelous people that they are. Were not we, sons and daughters of Nature and the Muse, (here the little fellow looked sharply and meaningfully at Haggard), willing to oblige and serve these Tewfik people, their life and work would be meaningless. We welcome you and have known that you would come. Rest now and in moments of time, the Tewfik will come to greet you."

Pleased with this kind of reception, we sit down on the ground. Cheese and bread and wine are there for us. Whether the elves have brought it, or whether we ourselves carried this in, I do not know, but there they are.

As I sit, it grows eerier. In my outer world, there is cold and rain. In the room in which I write, there is more cold and I feel the sense of isolation and aloneness. There is some resistance to going on with the tale, going on with the adventure in Tewfik Land. I feel the presence of Rider.

"What is this feeling of eeriness, Rider?" I ask. "Is it that the Tewfik are in danger of becoming too real?"

"No, I think not, Marvin. That is not troubling you. Such an event would excite you more than ever, as it would have me in my earth days. It is not that, I fear. Rather, I think that you are uncertain of your capacity to feel the reality of the Tewfik. You are worried lest the creative urge dry up. Yours is the concern of all writers, of fantasy or otherwise. Is not your book — and ours — entitled the Failed Writer or such? Are you not occupied with the problem of the writer who can not write or has no public, who has lost his speech, is uncertain of his talent or his message? Are you not preoccupied with all of this? That is partly why you attract me. For I, too, as I have said, want to relate writing and art to the life of the artist, fantasy to the occult, which is to say with the inner reality, with spirit and flesh, inside and outside. So, you are naturally concerned and fearful. But, it will flow. We, you and I, have been at home in the inner world of the soul, where fantasy dwells. And we both know that fantasy is also a real world. Come, let us allow the impossible to happen. Let us allow the flow to carry us, even now, as it carried us before, when we were in the boat on the river. Now that we walk amongst the green hills and glimpse another reality of white snow at the same time, let us flow with the river of events that appear to us. Remember, these Tewfik people honored you in your dream, did they not? Were you not a person of special merit? Why not trust that presentation of the fact and let us ..."

And now, while Rider was saying these last words, I caught a glimpse of a large man dressed in green. A Tewfik! Here he was, large and blond, with a hairy face but not a beard. He wore a green suit, like those of the middle ages, of Knights and such. Indeed, he reminded me of my dream long ago where I was initiated with branches of a tree at the hands of Knights. This green-robed fellow carried no emblem of a yellow lion or sun upon his chest, however, though he looked much like the Knights of that dream.

"I am no Knight," said the man, reading my thoughts, "but am a Tewfik, son of that proud nation of warriors and inspired ones. Indeed, your memory of that dream long ago, when you were but a youth, brought before a great assembly in order to be crowned — that memory of the dream is accurate, just as your last dream was also. We, the Tewfik, are the same in each dream. Separated, I think, by half a lifetime, more than twenty years, both dreams are true. It was we, the Tewfik, who were there to honor you, crown you, and you refused. Now, we honor you once more. Perhaps now you will be less modest, less fearful, and will be willing to take up the offer made you long ago."

"But who, indeed, are the Tewfik nation?" I ask. "Who are you to offer crowns, to wear green clothes of great radiance, to rule and make use of elves? Who are you to live on this beautiful green land, which is much like that of my friend here, Sir H. Rider Haggard? Do you know him as well?"

"We know him, as we know you. Indeed, he has already honored us more than once by ruling over us. Do you remember that, Sir H.? Do you recall that you, too, were our king?"

"I do not sir," responds Haggard. "I do not. If I did, it must have been in a dream, or a region of imagination that was not consciously available to me."

"But that is our realm, Sir Haggard! We are masters of the world of fantasy, in the Land of the Point, the node of the Pole, the imaginative place which unites the worlds. We are inspirers, as I have said. And warriors, too, as I also said. But this latter function may be more apparent to you later on. We are, most of all, servers of those who will serve us, as we serve the imaginative gods. Those who know the truth of the Border Land, those will we serve. In so serving, we serve ourselves. That is our task. We are the green ones, the nature ones, the wild ones of the soul. Haggard, you were here but did not realize it. But now coming as you do with this man, you will know it."

"I am perfectly willing," says Haggard.

"And I am willing also, but I am a little frightened again. Thoughts go through my mind of uncertainty, of self-deception, of poor writing, of inflation." These are my words to the Tewfik man.

"These are always thoughts of the writers and others who come here. It is strange that this is so, but true. You see one can not even come here until one has mastered the worlds of fantasy. One can not glimpse this place unless one has honored the soul, listened to its stirrings, married the Muse. We are the servers of the border region and only those who have already some achievement are permitted in. That you, Marvin, were offered the crown, long ago, was merely anticipatory of what would happen later. It was known that you would refuse, and that was right. You had to achieve much more in order to come here and rule in good conscience."

"But what does rulership mean? What does it mean to take up the crown? As I remember, that crown was huge, far greater than any human head could hold. In the years since, I have understood it as the symbol of Kether, the Kabbalistic Crown, where only the God who transcends all images and ideas dwells. That is where it touches the *Ain Soph,* the beyond."

"Yes, we are related to such images, to be sure, but that is not what we are about. Ours is a different slice of that same world, another dimension of thin paper in the great Book of the Worlds ... Do you not recall that in your dream of long ago you fought and slew the monster, the dragon who spit both red and yellow fire? Remember?"

"I do," I reply.

"Well, now you also know that it is the warrior in us who is also in you. You fought and slew the dragon of the fiery tongue. That is to say, you struggled with the demonic spirit of tongues, the creative word. That word, yellow with the gold of prophecy and intuition, red with the fire of emotion and passion, is what you defeated. And, in the defeating, capturing. The word, the word. Do you remember your stuttering silences of childhood? How you would not speak, nay, could not speak?"

"Yes."

"Well, even then you were being tested. Even then the words wanted to be spoken by you. But it needed years, those many years, until the dream. Many more years were needed until your pen and fingers spoke the words of the conquered dragon. Now, further years later, you once again come to the Land of the

Tewfik and are welcome to take up a place of honor and privilege. Yes, we understand you and know you, even if the larger world of concrete life does not. We not only understand you but have inspired you. All these years and words and images would have had no import, if not with the blessing of the Muse, whom we also serve."

I saw Haggard smile at this point and grow more interested. I had a hunch that the Muse ruled these people, that she was their queen, much as Haggard's *She* ruled both his stories and his soul. But I was quickly to be relieved of this intuition, because the Tewfik man shook his head negatively. I knew that he, like Haggard, had telepathic connection with my thoughts, so I was not surprised. But, becoming more aware of it, I ceased putting my question verbally and merely thought, What then, Tewfik? Who rules this green and fertile land?

"You do," came the answer, "or will, if you accept."

"What are the monarchical duties of this place?" I ask.

"They are many," he replied. "But the first of these is to write, to dedicate oneself to the images, ideas and feelings which emanate from here. Our first aim is to express. If you become monarch, you are to agree to this."

"I seem to have agreed to this in the past without being a monarch over anything, so I don't know what is new now!"

"A conscious commitment is what we ask. One in writing itself," responded Tewfik.

"I can do that," I reply, "provided that what emerges is truly creative, interesting, nourishing of the soul."

"Agreed," says the Tewfik man. "There shall be other *provisos* as well. But let me take you now to Tewfik Castle."

"All right," I reply, "But may I have a few words with my friend, Haggard?"

"You are King here, or almost," says the Tewfik man, "So you decide!"

I return to Haggard to talk with him. Before I do so, I remember that this Tewfik man has telepathic connection with me, so I make the sign of the Kabbalistic Cross and say the prayer proper to it:

"Atoh, Malkuth, ve Gedulah, ve Geburah, Le'olam, A-O-Men."

Which is to say: "Thou art the Kingdom, and the Glory, and the Power, Forever and Ever, Amen." After which I make a circle about myself and say: "The Tewfik are not yet permitted to communicate with me telepathically at their will. Not until I have given my full consent."

Then I turn to Haggard and ask him if all this seems right to him? Haggard nods; it seems quite all right. He does not remember having been in this land, let alone having ruled it, but he can accept the real possibility that he did so without being aware of it. He was, in point of fact, quite a master of the fantasy world and totally devoted to its expression. So there seemed no disparity here in what was said. In point of fact, since I, Marvin, had also been devoted to the same "Land" for many years but in a different way, there was no reason now to doubt it. In any case, I had the power to close off my own thoughts if I wished.

Well, I thought that Haggard was quite sensible, but then I had further worries about being a king of this land. What did it entail? I recalled other stories from other masters and mistresses of the imaginative realm, that Kings Must Die. Some kings were kings only for a day or a year and were then ritually sacrificed. Was this in store for me? I could not tell. But Haggard was here, and my silent friend, the Steersman. That fellow, with his dark and angelic powers, could probably save us if mischief came about. And wasn't he connected with that other King, He who sat in Judgment?

Should the Tewfik prove to be less than friendly, we had other powers as well. So then, good. And now I did a Kabbalistic Cross again, removing the Circle of Protection.

At that moment, I remembered another dream, one occurring before the great dream of the crowning. It was, perhaps, a year before. In it I came to a beautiful house which was like a castle, situated in a beautiful green field. Before I went near that castle, I made a magic circle around myself. End of dream. Now I understood that dream. I had touched the center of the magic land of vision and dream and creative expression, but there was danger in being lost. Even before I knew what magic really was, I was doing it. That spoke of knowledge I did not know that I possessed. There were parts of my soul that knew that which I did not know. A half-lifetime later I have uncovered much of that, and now these strands are coming together. Perhaps, I

speculated, this crowning and rulership have to do with coming
to be master of all those strands, all those pieces and fragments
of my soul that I have searched after, struggled with, and related
to all these years. Perhaps now, at last, I will come to myself, be
master of my own land, and be crowned with that sense of
wholeness and achievement ... These thoughts calmed me. And
this, along with Haggard's sensible words, his presence and that
of the Steersman, gave me courage to assent to the Tewfik man's
request. I agreed to accompany him to the castle. But, following
my memory of the dream long ago, I made a magical circle about
myself and my friends, Haggard and the Steersman.

So off we went toward the castle. The elves danced merrily
about us as we walked — a masculine quaternity: Haggard, the
Tewfik man, the Steersman, and myself. We walked in a sunset-
colored light, though no sun was apparent in that green land as it
darkened. We walked to the castle beyond.

"Sir Henry, are you there? Are you ready for us to continue
on our trip to the castle of the Tewfik people?"

"I am here. How is it that you do not question whether the
Steersman is there or not? You seem to count on him."

"True," I said. "I suspect that he will always be there. Is he
not an angel and a spirit, a Mercurial person who accompanies us
whether we will it or not? Is he not a representative of God
Himself? 'God is there, summoned or not,' goes a favorite
expression of mine, and here is his representative; not gaudy, not
overtly powerful, not even loving and trustworthy, but he is
there."

"Well spoken, Marvin. You recall that I said to you that you
trusted, even when you thought that you did not. Well, in that
little speech you have demonstrated the truth of what I have said.
You trust in the spirit, you trust in the subtlety of being led. You
trust, even, that God's angel does not necessarily mean to help
you all the time, but you trust that he/it is always there. Not
many men have felt that all their lives, now have they?"

"No, I suppose not."

"And it is a great gift and joy, is it not?"

"Yes, I suppose it is."

"Even in times of travail and despair, even when one feels
abandoned, stupid, brutalized, the angel is always there; the
Steersman of God is always there."

"Yes."

"Therefore have you been chosen, as you said. Not out of love nor virtue, but just because. Correct?"

"Correct."

"And just because of this closeness, have I asked and demanded and shown you that you, too, can choose. Correct?"

"Yes, correct."

"And that you chose me."

"Yes."

"And, in that, you are like God."

"Yes."

"And have power."

"Yes."

"Good. Then do not forget it, and let us be on our way to the castle."

Now, so instructed and reminded by my friend, Sir H. Rider Haggard, I find myself with him, Steersman, and the Tewfik man, walking along the road to the castle. It is dark and cold as we walk, the grass moist, the wind chilling. When we arrive at the castle, we are unable to see it in the dark night, but are immediately brought into a large room which is clearly a bath. It is tiled in a vine-design and contains several large pools: one steaming, one cold, along with several others. This room seems more like a Persian bath than a place of Northern people, but we do not complain. Rather, we quickly doff our clothes and seat ourselves in the hot water, enjoying the heat and feeling the gradual softening of our stiff muscles. I half expect some maidens to serve us, but there are none. We are alone in this room. Our needs in towels and soap are provided, but no people appear. The Tewfik man rejoices with us in the hot bath. He sits languidly at one end of a tub and seems lost in his dreams. I am tempted to go from hot to cold to hot again, but seeing that the others just relax and nod in the warmth of the room and its moist heat, I do the same.

I note that all are absorbed in fantasy, as if they have taken some potion or weed to induce it. But they have not. It is only the heat and moisture and relaxation which sends them off into their dreamland. I wonder, again, about fantasy within a fantasy. Two realities. We had just left off wondering about the two real-

ities of Tewfik Land itself, that of the Green and that of the Ice.
Not having yet seen the latter, I let myself enjoy the former.

But I cannot. I look about and see my friends relaxed, eyes
closed. But I cannot relax. Is that my fate? Is that my rigid stance
in life, to be ever in search, ever in conflict and desire? Am I
always to be dissatisfied? I sigh and feel the beginnings of tears,
but none fall. I attend to my body and try to coax it to relax. It
will not. And I must accept that it will not. Rather than disturb
my friends, however, I close my eyes and welcome fantasy.

Very quickly, I see a man alone on a desert, walking. I think
again of Haggard's Alan Quartermain, and of the heavy desert
journey in *King Solomon's Mines*. But this man is not a
Quartermain, I think. He seems to be both a nobody and
Everyman. He walks, step after step, and I see khaki trousers and
feet. As I raise my eyes further, I see a khaki shirt and then a
head of a thin, dark man, with a long neck and a large Adam's
apple. He has big dark eyes which look quite intense, but not
fierce. The man is of a Mediterranean race, but whether Spaniard
or Greek, Arab or Jew, is not clear. As I look at him, I remember
a man who looked something like him.

It was at a resort, I recall, in Southern California. I had gone
there with my mother when I was perhaps seven or eight years
old, during the school year. My mother was recovering from an
illness and I was brought along for a week or two because no one
else could take care of me. I enjoyed the place, with its trees,
nature, and quiet country-feeling, but I was much alone. At this
resort — Paradise was its name, most remarkably — there was a
man who looked like this fellow. He wore only khaki pants or
shorts and lived amidst the fruit trees and chickens and cacti at
the back of the resort. He was some sort of caretaker. I remember
talking with him and learning that he was not only a vegetarian,
but ate only raw, green salad. Everything else, he said, was like
poison. He had been near death, he said, had recovered, and now
lived in the most simple manner. He was very much alone, meditating (at this time, in my childhood, no one had ever spoken of
such a thing). I thought this man strange, but interesting. He
seemed to have something ...

And now, this man who is trudging the desert, walking on the
heated sands, in great thirst, reminds me of him. If, however, he
is Everyman, then my remembered friend of the resort is far dif-

ferent. Or if they are the same, in what way? Is it that we are all doomed to wander in this life, in the heat and dryness, longing for a cool drink to refresh us? Are we doomed to seek our treasure and spend long stretches in barren effort, feeling defeated? Yes, I suppose so. But as I looked at this man walking in the heat, I became aware that moments before we were in the cold of nature and then enjoyed the heat of baths. Now this man, suffering from the heat of nature, would enjoy something cool. I stop him therefore and give him a cool drink of water.

He did not see me. Indeed, he still does not see me. I become aware that I am just a mere hand who brings this watercan to him. At first he is only involved in drinking. Once that is accomplished, he looks in my direction with fear and astonishment. I become aware that he thinks me a god or demon who has come into his world.

"Have no fear," I say to this dark man. "I am not an angel nor a demon. I am only a being from another dimension who can visit you and see what you are doing."

"But you can read my mind, you can produce water out of nothing, and you are there in the air, with wings, and are so huge that I can hardly stand to look at you without falling to the ground in a faint."

This response of the man startles me. I look at my sides to see if I have wings, but I do not. Nor do I seem so huge. I can understand that he sees me above him, which is where I entered his space, but I seem no larger than he is. I am puzzled by this discrepancy, but decide to comfort him. I drop down to his ground and stand there. Now to my chagrin I am aware that I do, indeed, wear wings! For God's sake, I think, how in the Hell did I get to have wings? Am I an angel in his realm and quite a pained mortal in my own? The man still looks at me in dismay. He drops to the sand, bending his knees and bowing his head. He rocks back and forth, as if he were a Muslim at prayer.

I repeat to him, now touching his head: "Have no fear. I will not harm you. What I said to you is true. I can see that I do have wings, but I was not aware of it, because in my own dimension I do not have them."

The poor man looks up, less fearful now. He says: "You do look kindly, sire, and you have indeed brought me water. What do you wish of me?"

In truth, I was not aware that I wished anything of this man. I do know that he reminded me of a childhood memory however, and I tell him that. "And who are you?" I ask.

"I am Habib," he answers. "I wander here in search of a treasure which was said to have existed long ago, from the vast wealth of the King of the Hebrews, of Solomon, himself."

I am startled by this revelation. I wonder if the reality created by Haggard in his book has its own continuity, its own dimension, which can then be populated by other beings. Or did that reality already exist and was discovered in imagination by Haggard? In any case, what relation did this man have to my image from childhood?

"Do you know of a place ..." I begin, thinking to tell him about the resort of my childhood, but I realize that this would be impossible for him to reply to. I do not know what to do with him. Perhaps nothing. The man waits patiently. I touch him once again, on the shoulder, and he swoons to earth. I seem to have powers over him.

Puzzled by this experience, I open my eyes in the baths of the Tewfik and see my companions there, each with eyes closed and each, no doubt, either in his own fantasy or sleeping. I call out to Haggard and the Tewfik man, that I have had a strange experience. The Steersman opens his eyes of his own accord and smiles at me in a most strange way. I do not know what he is thinking. I tell Haggard and the Tewfik man of this strange encounter with Habib in my fantasy, who thought I was an angel. Haggard says that, yes, he thought that he did not invent the desert land of *King Solomon's Mines,* but that he discovered it. The whole experience of writing that book, with its swiftness, its flow, its independent reality, was such that he half-believed, at the time, that there was an autonomous existence which he had contacted. But he had never thought of himself as an angel. That would be too much! The Tewfik man nodded understanding and, although he said nothing, I got the impression that this was a valid experience of mine; that once I was a true member of Tewfik land, I would have contact with many dimensions of life and being, that in some I would appear as a god, in others as a slave or ant. This was as it should be. How else could a Tewfik, resident of the land of Muse and prophecy, fantasy and invention, be?

The response of the Steersman was even more shaking. He merely looked at me with his dark face and penetrating eyes and smiled that strange smile. I remembered that I had experienced him as an angel and that I had behaved with him rather like Habib had behaved with me. Was it possible that the Steersman, in his own realm, was no angel? But I had seen him there, at the Throne of Judgment; I had seen him change form and being. I had known him in his mercurial form as a changeling, I had ... Well, what? Perhaps I could no more comprehend his reality than Habib could comprehend mine. I knew that I could play with Habib, tease him, fool him, or give him boons. Perhaps the Steersman could and would do the same with me. Why should I be benevolent to Habib and why should the Steersman be so with me?

With these thoughts, I turned to Tewfik Man and Haggard hoping for some help from them, but they seemed to have no more to say. So then I speak to the Steersman:

"Are you, Sir, to me as I am to Habib?"

The Steersman nods.

"Are you not an Angel then, but from another dimension?"

The Steersman nods once more.

"Well then, what am I to do? Merely accept this? I ..."

And then I have no words. In some ways, of course, the Steersman is far superior to me in his changing capacity, his relation to the Throne, his quiet comfort with what is; just as I am superior to poor Habib over there in that other dimension. But what should I do? It is a strange and unexpected dilemma, a weird thing to happen as soon as I find myself in the castle of the Tewfik. Shall I instruct or be instructed? Shall I take Habib with me to Tewfik land and really drive him mad? Will this not be like the tales of the space men appearing on earth and taking poor earthlings for a ride? Goodness, why should I do this? Better, I shall ask old Habib what he would like! This could be good preparation for my assuming an angel-like status, a powerful role as a monarch of Tewfik land. Let me then try my hand as an Angel. With these thoughts, I return to Habib and touch him once again. He awakens.

"What would you desire, Habib?" I ask. "Name it and I shall produce it for you."

Habib looks at me in wonder, saying "Make it green here."

"Easily done," say I. I wave my hand and make this desert look much like the land of the Tewfik. Habib is astonished and looks terrified again. His eyes then narrow and he says, "Bring me the treasure of King Solomon."

Again with the merest wave and thought on my part, I produce for him a large chest, containing much gold and jewels. His eyes pop out, but he is again terrified. He scoops out a few pieces of gold and jewels and begins to run. Soon he leaves the green which I had created for him, running back to the desert, toward an unknown city or village from whence he came. I could, of course, follow him, but I do not choose to. Instead, I consult with my friends.

"You have much to learn about the uses of creative power," says the Tewfik Man smiling, but hinting all the same that there is, indeed, much I have to learn.

"Now you know," says the Steersman, adding nothing more.

Now, indeed, I do know, think I, but I am not sure what it is that I know. I realize that what is God or Angel at one level, is merely human and mortal at another. Most of all, I realize that I know less than I thought. Where now is my understanding? It has left me and it seems futile. What does it matter if these worlds are seen as "levels of fantasy"? What does it matter if Habib is a fragment of my own unconscious and the Steersman is, in truth, a ruling spirit? I now experience them both differently and thereby everything is changed. What if, indeed, Haggard is only my own inner "writer" taking objective form? What if? It does not seem that way and Haggard himself promised to prove his independent reality to me. And what of the Tewfik man? I am confronted with so many types of psychic reality and concrete reality, too, that I am confused. Is that what it means to be a resident of Tewfik Land? I suppose it is.

These thoughts having rested a bit in my relativized mind, I could now turn to my friends and ask them what form of thought or fantasy was taking place with them while I was discovering my angelhood with Habib in the Haggardian Desert. Sir H. Rider Haggard responds first when I ask my question.

"It is strange that you should ask that question, Marvin, and it is stranger still that I must answer it. When you were in communication with Habib, you were no longer in telepathic union with me. At that moment, I was about my own business, not focused upon you at all, nor were you on me. Hence our psychic realities were separated and a gap occurred. There is something for me to learn in that. Continuity seems to mean focus, and memory seems to hinge upon attention. And when I tell you where I was in my fantasy, you will be even more astonished, because it goes even further on the path to confusion. As you were talking to Habib, thinking that he reminded you of your experience of that dark man of your childhood, I was having a pleasant experience in the tub — of warmth and relaxation — and then thought of the desert of *King Solomon's Mines*. In that, therefore, we were — you and I — both focused upon a common reality, but unknowingly, synchronistically perhaps. But then I became aware of a dark man sitting in a meditative position in a pleasant sort of spot, near fruit trees, cacti and chicken pens. This man, I now realize, is the same whom you knew in your earlier childhood and to whom you associated the experience of Habib. Now I was in some sort of contact with him, though I did not know that he came from — or had a relation with — your experience. I merely saw this man meditating and I was aware of what was going on in his fantasy. I saw a plate of greens, for example, which he apparently was looking forward to. I also saw an attractive group of women, houris perhaps, dressed in silken pants, wearing thin veils. They were dancing and my meditative person was hungrily thinking of them.

"At this point, I was startled by this, thinking it strange that I was having a fantasy of a man having a fantasy, but I accepted it. Then the man opened his eyes, as if to say, 'Who is here? Who is intruding into my mind?' I tried to reassure the fellow, mentally communicating that I only happened upon him and did not intend to disturb his privacy. But this act of calming, much like your act of calming with Habib, only managed to disturb him more."

"Who are you," he asked, "and what are you doing here in my mind? I did not summon you nor did I acknowledge an openness to you."

"Naturally, I was unable to answer the man, although now I had at least an idea that what was happening was, in part, an intermingling of the psychic reality of the two of us, Marvin, in a manner different than before. I was unknowingly in touch with a memory of yours which seems to have continued onward in a creative way, inhabited by a person of some reality, and you were in touch with my creative image of the past, but meeting a person who was totally unknown to me. More than that I can not say. But, to continue with my experience of the meditative person, I told him that I was a writer, having written books that he might have known of and that I was dead in one dimension, alive in another. The man answered that he knew nothing of life or death; as far as he was concerned this all was illusion and that the only reality was the non-reality of peaceful meditation. I was apparently some ghost, some maya-like demon who came to disturb him in his serenity. Not wishing to disturb him further, I said that if he wished me to leave, I would indeed be a cooperative demon and leave. This seemed to give him some satisfaction, as if he were a kind of Buddha, able to drive off the *devas* of ignorance. So I returned my attention to this place, just when you were raising your questions. If you were an unexpected Angel in a land which I 'created,' then I was a Demon in a memory land of yours which no longer exists! These changes rather boggle the mind, I am afraid. Perhaps, the Tewfik Man here can offer us an explanation."

I was amused by Haggard's story and felt a certain symmetrical justice in it, but was not expecting the Tewfik Man's answer.

"Despite my extensive knowledge and experience of Tewfik life," he said, "I must confess that I can not answer you at this time, Sir Haggard. Indeed, during the period of the quiet time shared by all of us, I myself had an experience which was new to me. As I lay peacefully in my bath, enjoying the heat and pleasant sensations of the water — just as you did, Haggard — I found myself in a cold, icy region which I suddenly and shiveringly (not from cold but from awe) recognized as the 'underside,' so to speak, of Tewfik Land, that is to say, Tewfik Iceland. I had always known that the other condition of Tewfik Land was that of ice and there are many stories among our people about our sister State, but I had never before been privileged to visit this place. I knew that I was now there, but I did not know why this was so nor what I was to do there. I felt the cold of the snow, the wind blowing mightily, but was also aware of a peculiar light. It was intense and bright, yellow in color. This light emanated from the ice itself and it felt as if it pulled upon or attracted the green light which we of Tewfik Land give off and which seems natural to us. As I felt this pull of the yellow light, I also felt a kind of gravitation, as if the ice were pulling me into itself. I was gradually drawn down and grew colder and colder. I was pinned, like a great lead weight, to the ice land itself. As the pull grew heavier, I sensed that the green light was going out of me — or my clothes — and that I was being reduced to a pitiful, naked, mortally fleshly condition. I could not understand this. How was this so? I, an important figure and noble of Tewfik Land, with a mission of value, an energy of note, and a spiritual beauty, was now being bereft of all my virtue, becoming not only like the living mortal here, Marvin, but worse, rather feeble, naked, and impotent at that! Why? Was this not Tewfik Land also? And why did our stories speak of the value of Tewfik Iceland and not tell us Tewfik people of the reduction that we would experience when transported there?

"Well, as I pondered this question and felt myself shrinking even in size, I now saw — way down below the Iceland of Tewfik — a big dark man, with a large Adam's apple. He was dressed either in the white shirt and slacks of Hindus or a kind of khaki. He looked at me with a smile and then promptly appeared as far above me, in the air, as he had below me a moment before. His words to me were few. He merely said, 'Now you understand what it means to be a mortal man. Until now you have only guessed about mortal man's life. You have guided and inspired him, but only when he was summoned or chose to see you and your people — that is to say, when he was gifted himself. But now you see the underside of that state, which is feeble, delicate, vulnerable, and pathetic. You learn this only by experiencing the opposite of your light, just as you experience the opposite of your condition. So then, give thanks to the mortal man who is there with you, for it is by his lights that your lights are broadened!' After that he vanished, as if he were some Jinn, such as we here are quite familiar with.

"That was my experience. A moment later, I was called to a consciousness of us all here. And it was only as you two spoke, Marvin and Haggard, that I understood what had happened to me. This dark man, so feeble in your experience, Marvin, and so meditative in yours, Haggard, was a true Jinn in mine! Whether this was all some variation of the same person, relative to the condition of each of us, or whether these are truly different creatures from different dimensions, I can not say. I can only say that now I have been to the other side of Tewfik Land, I know the Ice thereof, and I know what it means to be mortal!"

Haggard and I looked at each other a little astonished. We were by no means so impressed with the value of knowing what it means to be mortal, having suffered that fate, but we were both struck that not only we as mortals were gaining new experience and insight by our adventure, but that an immortal, like the Blond man of Tewfik Land, with his heroic appearance and being, could learn something, even if only what it is like to be mortal. Yet he acknowledged that he had never been to the underside of Tewfik and it was our presence which facilitated it. It was that dark figure who made that pronouncement. We were still in the dark, I thought, about who that dark figure was: Habib the Weak, Habib the Meditative Man, or Habib the Jinn. Then Steersman spoke up:

"Perhaps my own experience will add to your collective enlightenment, gentlemen. Since I am no mortal, have never been one, living nor dead, and since I am also no Muse-Server, such as is Tewfik Man here, perhaps I can bring some light to bear which is different from all of yours. It is neither green, like that of Tewfik, nor yellow, like that of the dark man, nor is it the softer, candle-like light of you mortals. It is white. Pure white. As we all settled into the enjoyment of the baths — and I, too, can enjoy such things, even though I do not partake of mortal being — I felt called upon to return to the side of my King at the Center of Judgment. That is my home, at the side of my Lord, and that is the source of my being. So when I am not needed nor involved in the dimensions appropriate to you all here, I naturally gravitate there. I found myself once again at the Throne of Being and felt the flow of white light between the Ancient One, Blessed be His Name, and myself. I felt the energy flow out of me back into Him, just as the energy of the lion flowed into me, leaving the sender in each case only the merest shell and form. Now, in this flowing, I felt aware of a certain tension, pain, and rigidity which remained with my form. I did not know why. I had not before been aware of this rigidity, pain and tension. Then, I became aware of the pain and tension of the mortal, Marvin, as he sat there with us in the baths, unable to free himself from his pressure and mortality. He felt, of course, that this was because of the all-too-fleshy limitation of his muscles and bones. But at that moment, I became conscious that it is not just the limits of muscle and bone which mortals feel, but the limitation of form itself! It is form which constrains, narrows, contains and, in the containment, is both creative and killing. It is form which brings pain. We only know this when we leave form and flow back into the uncontained, formless God of creation.

"At that moment, too, I was aware of the special relation between myself, the mercurial and changeable, divine and paradoxical angel experienced by you, Marvin, and the permanent, unchanging, divine throne from which I come and to which I go. It is as if I adore myself and create myself when I am there, and that I deceive myself and lead myself when I am here. The pain, however, comes from the form. We suffer it. Free from the form — free from the pain."

"But," ask I, Marvin, upon hearing this revelation from the mercurial Steersman, "what is your intention in all this? And what of that dark one, called Habib, Meditative One, and Jinn by all of us here, we who have form and are mortal and immortal, living and dead? What of that?"

"Our intention is creation itself, for itself. And, as to the dark one, do you not know him?"

At this point, the Steersman smiles and quickly shifts his being to a form of Habib, then the Meditative Man, and the Jinn. He laughs and returns to being the dark Steersman at our side. I realize then that the Steersman, the mercurial one, is the great leader and hinderer. He, the representative of the great unchanging God is the changing God. He is all around us, at every level of being and every dimension thereof, in fact and fiction, memory and creation, above and below. And now we, Haggard and Tewfik Man and myself, realizing with whom we are conversing, fall to the ground, just as Habib did, and worship this Angel.

He laughs, does the Steersman, and we laugh too.

We have laughed, all of us, and are filled with good spirits, but now we are aware of a new presence in these Persian-like baths. In the steamy room, in the light-reflected warmth of the flowered, moist tiles, we are suddenly confronted with a feminine presence. Before there was none, but now we sense a woman. She sits, this woman, there in another bath, her knees supporting a head covered with orange-red hair.

How did she come there, this woman? And who is she? Is she a citizen of Tewfik Land? But before I can ask this question of our Tewfik host, the Blond Man in Green, I feel compelled to stare at this woman. She gives off an intense orange light. A flesh-colored energy radiates from her as she sits there, folded in upon herself. She is dressed in a sheer silken, tight-fitting, orange gown. Who is this woman? Is she the Muse that Haggard hinted about and wanted us to visit? I turn now to my friends — Haggard, Steersman, and Tewfik Man — to see what they have to say about this presence.

Haggard stares at her, just as I did. The Steersman looks away and seems present to other realities than occupy me at this moment. The Tewfik Man also stares at our visitor.

"Do you know who she is?" I query of Haggard and the green-clothed Tewfik. They both shake their heads.

"She is not of our nation," says the Tewfik. "We are blond and green-clothed, green-lighted, here."

"Nor is she the Muse," says Haggard. "At least not as I have known her in my lifetime — or deathtime, for that matter," he continued, as he smiled.

"I wonder then," say I, "who she is, how she got here?"

I get out of my bath, wrap a towel about my middle, and go toward this unknown woman. As I approach her, I not only sense the brightness of the orange light which emanates from her, but I also begin to smell a strong, fleshy body odor, which is at first delicate and attractive, but which then becomes almost overpowering; I do not know if I like it.

Now, close to her, I do not know what to do. My friends stay in the background, content for me to do the investigating in this matter. My nose is filled with her scent, my eyes become watery with her light, yet I try to reach her with a human and polite greeting. "How do you do? May I ask who you are, and why you are here?"

The woman looks up for a moment and reveals a finely chiseled face with thin nose, delicate lips, along with soft bright eyes which do not express any particular mood. She looks at me for a moment and then, unanswering, resumes her apparent meditation with her head on her knees. I do not know what to say next, but am tempted to touch her attractive body, to stroke those thighs, covered by the stocking-like gown that she wears, but I restrain myself, of course.

"Why, 'of course'?" the woman says, looking up. "You do not automatically restrain yourself with women, I imagine, but take your pleasures whenever you can."

I am only a little startled by this woman reading my thoughts, since that seems to have been the pattern of many of the people that I have met in my adventure thus far: the Steersman and Haggard for example, but not the Tewfik Man, I think. Nor, to think of it, have Steersman and Haggard been routinely able to read my thoughts. No, only when I have consciously or unconsciously permitted it, have they done so. Yet, this woman seems to have read them. She knew "of course," but she did not and does not know about my restraint or non-restraint. Actually, she is making a judgment about me and my behavior by guessing. I tell her this, but she merely shrugs and resumes her head-on-knees position.

Well then, think I: what does she want? Is she judgmental of me, accurate or inaccurate? Seems so, but why?

"Why, indeed," she looks up again, sighs, and resumes her, by-now-irritating, position.

"You seem to want to relate to me only on your own terms," I retort rather angrily, "and I don't like it!"

Now the orange lady looks up again and smiles. She seems to be pleased at my getting angry with her. "At last I finally got some attention from you," she says, without irritation or peeve, rather good-naturedly, open-faced.

"You gentlemen," she continues, addressing us all, "different as you are, all seem quite pre-occupied with questions of spirit and form, creation and flow, mind and matter. At no point have I heard any mention of flesh, of love, of being-in-itself, not as Idea. I have hardly even heard mention of feelings."

"I acknowledge that to be true, Madam," say I, "but why should you be interested and how did you come here? Tewfik Man does not know you to be of this land, and yet you are."

"The Tewfik Man knows only the Green of Tewfik. Lately, as a result of your visit, he has come to know the White Ice of

Tewfik Land, that which his tales and myths have spoken of, but which he has never experienced. Further, that taught him a bit of what mortality and life feels like. But he saw only a piece of the Tewfik Land of Ice. There is more to Tewfik than he knows of, and that is the Land of the Orange. We of the Orange are as much a part of Tewfik Land as is your blond and handsome green man. Can you not tell that we, too, are Tewfik? Do we not, also, give off a glow of light, every bit as intense as that of the blond man, although ours is orange and not green? It is true, I will hasten to inform you, in answer to my rhetorical question. It is also true that we are as far from the mortals as are the people of Green Tewfik Land, but we are, one might say, spirits of the flesh. We are, in every way, more fleshy, more earthy, more sensual, more human than human — if one can use such an expression — without being human ourselves. Tewfik-Green is terribly proud of creativity, of honoring and serving poets and artists. Of course, and is right to be. But we of Tewfik-Orange are creative in the flesh — or actually, of the precursors of the flesh. How do you imagine flesh life gets its reality, creativity, if not from us? We are, you might say, the archetypes of the flesh and in that no less creative and spiritual than any other part of Tewfik Land. For us, your struggles with lions, with images, with questions of reality, seem rather amusing."

"But why," I ask, a little surprised but pleased with her long speech, "are you here at all?"

"Because you wanted it, dear man. Can you not tell this yet? You have come to Tewfik Land because you were informed that you were honored here. Well, not only Tewfik Green honored you because you have served the creative spirit of imagination. We of Tewfik Orange have honored you because you have served the spirit — the spirit, mind you — of the creative flesh. That you have done, as you well know, with passion, tenderness, questioning, and devotion. To serve the spirit of the flesh is as great an achievement as to serve the spirit of fantasy. It is this for which I come here to honor you. That one," she says, pointing to Haggard, "I dare say, is also honored in Tewfik Land, but not by us."

This speech completed, I looked at Haggard, who continued to be startled and a little aghast. This was something that he had not anticipated. He was surely a leader as an artist and creative

man, as well as successful in the world — in contrast to my fate
as a "failed artist" — but he did not know of the spirit of the
flesh, it seems, at least according to this lady. He did not recognize this woman at all, and denied that she was a Muse.

Haggard, gentleman and fine person that he was, recovered
himself at last and nodded toward the woman and me. "You are
right, Madam," he said, "you are right." And then to me, "Marvin, this is indeed unexpected for me as an artist; but as a man
interested in the occult, I find this most interesting. The flesh and
its connection with the subtle body and matter itself, as moved
by the spirit, was of central interest to me as a man and as one
fascinated by the occult. Perhaps now I shall indeed learn more."

This generous response and appreciation was just what I
would have expected from the kind of man I imagined Haggard
to be: a gentleman, intelligent, sensitive, and open. The Tewfik
Woman nodded also in appreciation of his remarks. The
Steersman turned his eyes toward the woman and smiled. Only
Tewfik Man remained startled and open-mouthed.

"This is too much," he said, shaking his head, "too much.
Here you come to our land, Marvin, to be honored by us,
instructed by us, and to ultimately rule over us, and already I
have been taught by your presence. As a consequence of your
being here, I have visited the Ice Land of Tewfik, have experienced the Yellow and Golden Light, have felt what it is to be
mortal, and now meet with a whole new branch of my own
nation that I had never known! I have heard stories about the
Orange-Red folk, but no one that I have ever known has actually
experienced such a person or place. And now I see her, and 'in
the flesh,' as a mortal might say. I wonder then, who is to be
teacher and who is to be taught!"

"Perhaps we all are," I answered jocularly, but really believing that is how things really ought to be between the world of
spirits and the world of mortals. We mortals should, by now,
give up our bad habit of merely kowtowing to the spirit-world or
pooh-poohing it. When we relate more equally, all worlds are
changed, I would imagine. I add the "I would imagine," only
because I have, indeed, been able to change only the world of
fantasy, not the world of flesh or matter. Thus my excitement
and interest in meeting with this woman of Orange-Red Tewfik
Land, who claims to be of the spirit of flesh. Perhaps here par-

ticularly my understanding and power can be enhanced. Perhaps here I can continue my quest to change my condition from Failed Artist to Realized Artist. If the Spirit of the Flesh cannot help me in this task, then who can? And if I cannot become the Successful Writer, then perhaps I can become a Whole one in spirit and in flesh. She and they of Orange-Red Tewfik Land honor me. Well! We shall see what that entails.

... A few days have gone by, and I now seem to be alone in Tewfik Land. I do not see the Tewfik Man, Haggard, or the Steersman. I do, however, sense the Tewfik Orange-Red woman, as she sits there with her head on her knees, lost in thought. I am not aware at this moment of the intense emanation of color and light from her as I did before. Instead, I experience a gnawing in my belly: a vague sensation of unease or hunger, which could change into sadness or restlessness at any moment. But I do have a clear sense that this condition in my belly is directly related to her, either caused by her or something she would understand, have power over, or both. Indeed, I would guess that her red-orange light has, in fact, entered my being at the region of my navel and quietly churns my belly there.

The Orange-Red Tewfik Woman looks up and smiles, showing a delicate, sensitive face, features that one might not expect from an archetypal spirit of flesh and sensuality, but there it is. As she smiles, I feel less pain in my belly and want more to weep than to eat. I think of my life-long struggle with hungers for food, for drink, for sex, for everything. I think of my perennial battle with excess, with the desire to be in good shape, and with the spirit. As I think of that, I look at the smiling Tewfik Woman.

"Why do you smile so sweetly, Madam?" say I. "If you do read my mind, then you know what I am thinking. You know about my struggles with the flesh, with the passions of desire and the swamps of despair that I fall into."

"I do know about them, yes," she says and grows silent.

I am reminded of a dream I once had. In it I came to a green land, much like Tewfik Land, in which was situated a beautiful

monastery made of white stone. The field in front of the monastery was sometimes green and carefully trimmed with manicured
lawns, well-tended trees and flowers. At other times, it was like a
swamp: very wet and muddy, but with rice and other things
growing there. At the moment of the dream, I was informed that
an exchange was taking place: a monk, having lived many years
in the monastery, was now getting ready to go into the world. At
the same time, a business man, successful and experienced in the
world, was about to enter the monastery. A flow from one to the
other, from extraversion to introversion, and the reverse; from
spirit to flesh and the opposite. Just as the flow of men shifted, so
did the flow of nature: when the garden of the monastery was
green and beautiful with lawns and trees, it was aesthetic and
pleasing to the senses; when the garden was swampy and thick
with life, it was a source of food. End of dream.

But why, I thought, did I remember this dream now, as I stood
before the Tewfik Woman, mistress of the flesh? I looked to her
for an answer, but none came. She merely smiled prettily once
again and was silent. Then I realized that this dream was much
like what the Tewfik Woman had complained about when I
approached her before: all the concerns of Haggard, The Tewfik
Man, even the Steersman, were of the spirit and its changes of
form and meaning. Little attention was paid to the flesh, to pleasure, to being-in-itself. My dream was the same; it had to do with
the spirit and its changes. Yes, there was a sense of beauty and
hunger, even the sense of material success, but it was all in the
context of maleness and spirit.

"Yes," says the Tewfik Woman, reading my thoughts.

"But, Tewfik Woman," say I aloud, "then please read my
mind's flesh, my soul's desire, my agonized struggle with matter,
and tell me how ... when ... what, in short, I can do to end this
never-ceasing struggle, be at home with the flesh and spirit at the
same time? I beg you, please inform me."

"Changes, always changes," says the woman, cryptically.

What does she mean? Even the desire for change is non-flow,
non-accepting of the moment? Yes, I know. But I feel helpless to
change that or anything else! I sit down now and put my head on
my own knees and sigh. I copy the Tewfik Woman and retreat to
an inner world of hoped-for serenity. She merely laughs, not
meanly nor patronizingly, but with an amusement that is both

accepting and pitying. All right, that's how it is. So, I sit with my head upon my knees.

Now I feel her stroking my head and my neck, quite gently. I look up enquiringly. She just smiles softly. She closes my eyes with her fingers, soothingly touching the lids and lashes, as if freeing them of tension. I am transported, once again, into Orange-Red Tewfik Land. This happens not in a flash, but in stages. First I am outside the castle, then I am in the sunset-colored light which I experienced when all of us were approaching it and I was aware that this light was devoid of the sun. Now I find myself in a land where everything is of orange-red shades, it is sunset wherever one looks. But there is no sun. This, no doubt, was the place-time which was revealed on our walk to the castle and into which I was transported. Why did not the Tewfik Man know of this? And where are all my friends now? But forget these questions and see how it is to be in Orange-Red Tewfik Land.

I find myself in a place where the ground is soft to the foot and very sensual. It seems to be spongy, made of a substance like foam-rubber. As I walk about, my feet settle in, and the sensation is both pleasant and unpleasant. It is pleasantly soft, but unpleasant in the lack of change; there being no hard place at all. I walk around and I see no one and no thing. Not even the Tewfik Woman is there. Why not, I wonder, and where is she? I sit down once more and put my head on my knees. I try and let the whole world of Orange-Red Tewfik come into my being, soften up my hardness and pressured searchingness. But it does not happen, so I sit.

After a time, I notice a presence. I open my eyes and see that Sir H. Rider Haggard has also come here. He sits quietly next to me, in a meditative posture. I wonder if that is what has happened to him since experiencing the being which I called Habib, but for him was a kind of Hindu. But I say nothing, nor does he. In a while, there also appears in this place the blond Tewfik Man. He stands with arms folded across his chest, erect, as if he is firm in holding on to his own viewpoint. He is standing guard, perhaps, yet is in no way assertive or aggressive. At last, Steersman appears in this Orange-Red Tewfik Land. He squats, rests on his heels, and smiles. His smile, unlike that of the Orange-Red Woman, is neither amused nor pitying. Rather, the smile is one of friendship, knowing more, perhaps, than the rest of us, but unwilling to either offer this knowledge or to withhold it. Now that we are all there, then what? Nothing. Our multitude of maleness and spirit has no effect, it seems, on this cosmos of soft orange-redness. It just is. Best to just remain in our respective states, I think: Haggard meditating, Tewfik Man in a firm stance of guarding and self-esteem, the Steersman with humor, and I in my sadness and sense of defeat. Thus do we all, in our maleness, look at and deal with the land of Orange-Red Tewfik, the spirit of flesh.

... Sometime later, we are all still sitting there in the land of Tewfik Orange on the spongy ground, the orange-red light of continual sunset encircling us. There meditates Haggard, stands the Green-Tewfik Man, and amusedly squats the Steersman. But a change has occurred in me during this time. My friends are unchanged, but in the midst of stillness and the quiet surrender to being, sensual desire came over me. At first it was only a vague stirring, but then became clearly sexual, bringing images of the tender inside flesh of a woman's thighs, with soft and moist hair. The vision, orange and black, of thigh and hair, was deepened by the addition of smell. It was gentle and subtle, violent and gross, simultaneously. Attracted and repulsed these opposites were too much, could make me flee or fall into total abandon.

Now I felt another sense activated: touch. As I imaginally touched that soft thigh, the caress sent shivers into my hand, arm and shoulder. Yet another sense came in: I heard. What I heard was my own sigh. My breath let go and I heard a sigh of relaxation, as I sank into ecstasy.

But with whom was I having this experience, this fantasy of pleasure? The images shifted to those I have loved, to those with whom I have had such experiences, and then to those with whom I would have liked to have that experience. Once again I sighed, and once again I let go. But this time it was neither relaxation nor sweet surrender. Rather, it was with a further sense of defeat, of the inability of my spirit to remain faithful and true. I was not only a failed artist, but also a failed man of the spirit, whose highest principles and ideals had been defeated by flesh, by desire and hunger and passion. And, at times, defeated also by the death of desire! Old Mercurius may have been in it all along, but now I call out to the Woman of Orange-Red Tewfik Land:

"Oh, Orange Woman, Spirit of Flesh, as you and your *confreres* call yourselves, come and aid me now in my blockage and despair. Help me to feel at home with your spirit of flesh, to be at-one with it, so that these flights back and forth, these betrayals of one side or the other, will vanish from my field of vision."

Orange Tewfik Woman obliges and I watch her slowly incarnating herself before me, taking on increasing substance. At first slender, long-legged and small-breasted, she grows fuller, athletic, and firm. She transforms into all the women I have known. Is she a female version of Mercurius? Is she like my Lord and Angel of Change? Is she merely another manifestation of that wildly hermaphroditic substance-spirit being?

She merely smiles ... I draw forward to her and try to touch her. She leans forward as I touch her, but it is not the same — I do not sense her as I did before, not as I did when I was gripped with desire, enfolded in memory, overcome by the sensual reality of it. Now, there seems to be a weakening of the power of the image itself, a beginning of panic, a loss of my potent desires. I find myself desperate to maintain the desire not to lose that pleasurable possibility of joy, satisfaction, and release! Now I am more aware than ever of my own duplicity, my own mercurial attitude toward desire: fight it, block it, restrain it, and then quickly hold it, intensify it. Perhaps though, these are not so perverse after all, are they? Both attitudes want to prolong the desire and pleasure; maybe both want to include the spirit, somehow. But I am a loss. I long for the Orange Tewfik Woman to speak, inform me, to enhance my being with greater consciousness, quickened desire, deeper love.

"Easily done," says the Tewfik Woman. "Only allow the stimulation to be, the pleasure to exist. Let feeling flow, desire be. Do not fight it, nor analyze it. Do not spiritualize it. It just is, this spirit of flesh. Listen to each instance and you shall hear it, feel it, and enjoy it."

"But, what of the later effect, fair lady, when desire has been fulfilled or control has been lost, when the negative spirit of judgment intervenes and has its say: 'Betrayer of spirit, breaker of rules and hearts.' "

"Is that what it says, mortal man?"

"Yes."

"And what do you say?"

"I seem unable to answer its judgment. I fight feebly, collapse in surrender, and when desire resumes once again, go through the round of battle and defeat."

"So, the battle is of Judge and that-which-is-judged?"

"Yes."

"And each is equally powerful?"

"Yes."

"Now one wins, and then the other?"

"Yes."

"What is your position in this battle?"

"My position?" I ask, a little surprised. "My position? I seem to be the victim in it. I experience myself identified with now one and now the other. I try to bring them together, but often fail."

"Where, then, is the chooser?" she asks. "Where then is the heroic man that we of Tewfik, both Green and Orange, have called here to honor? Is it only a poor soul who is pushed about here and there? Have you no stance of your own?"

"Well, I have had, as you probably know. I have had a position which accepts the struggle, but this has not brought surcease, contentment, self-esteem, or union."

With my statement of the word, "self-esteem," the Tewfik Man, standing there with his arms folded across his chest, looks up interestedly. He says nothing, but is now involved and listening. I look to see what my other friends are thinking or feeling. Haggard is still in meditative repose. I am not sure if he hears what is going on or is engrossed in his own fantasy. The Steersman maintains his amused attitude, although he does seem to be more related to the conversation between the Orange Tewfik Woman and myself.

As I look at the Tewfik Man, I think of my struggle with self-esteem in this battle. Yes, the loss of self-esteem seems a very potent force. The Judge who can cause this sits upon his Throne and sends his energies into the Mercurial One and into me. I wonder what he wants of me?

"And what do you want, Mortal Tewfik Man?" says Orange Tewfik Lady.

I wonder why she calls me Tewfik Man, since I am not such a one. What do I want, indeed? I want my self-esteem, of course. I want that Judge upon the Throne to accept me. And I want, too, that the flow of energy, of love and life, be accepted also.

"Do you accept it, Tewfik Man?" says the Orange Lady.

"No, I do not," say I. "But why do you address me as a Tewfik Man? I am not one, as far as I know."

"You are. You are fickle, as you have noted before, and also of two fictions. The fiction of the one is the truth of the other. Did you not know this? What do you think the meaning of our Tewfik Land is, anyway? Is it not a duality and polarity? Why do you suppose that we, both Orange and Green Tewfik, honor you? Because you honor us or honor that which we honor? Yes, that is partly true, but it is also because you are like us: dual. You are like us: polar. We are of the polar regions after all, not one-sided, but two. But you are even more polar than we are. Green Tewfik, after all, knew nothing of mortality and even less of the Yellow Light, until you brought that. I am, in truth, a spirit of flesh, but you bring ... But I cannot yet say what you bring to us of Orange Tewfik. First, you must embrace your self-esteem. Embrace yourself, mortal man, and become a Prince of Tewfik! Embrace your duality and hold your self-esteem!"

"I seem not to be able to, dear Lady, neither in the flesh, nor in the spirit. Why, for example, am I so dependent upon my books seeing the fleshy world of the binding, of the bookshop, of the world? Why do I obsessively ruminate about success and failure, of recognition and oblivion, of status and the reverse? And why do I everlastingly search out Justice, and yet find it evanescent?"

"Why?" asks the Tewfik Orange Lady.

"I don't know," say I. "Only that I can not give myself self-esteem, but need it from other sources."

"Yes. And we here are intent on giving it to you."

"But, alas, your words do not give it to me, either. I feel myself, dear Lady, sinking back, falling into ..."

Nothingness. That into which I sink is nothingness. Non-being. But then I find myself flying. I leave the Lady, my friend Haggard, the Green Tewfik Man and the Steersman, and I fly up to the Throne once more. I fly up to the power of Judgment, the King, He-Whom-I-Cannot-Please, to my Self who is my hardest judge and severest critic. He is both mine, yet not mine at all, above and beyond me ...

At the Throne sits the Judge. He is old, grey, and bearded, just like everybody's ancient image of God the Father. This God the

Father, though, is not at all stern. He is smiling and amused. He seems even more benevolent than my friend and guide, Mercurius, the Steersman. I wonder why it is that I do not feel his blessing, his esteem of me.

"You have my esteem, mortal man," says the Judge. "I do not judge you harshly. You do. You, yourself."

"How can that be?" say I. "How can it be that I judge myself so harshly, when I experience that harsh Judge to be you?"

"I cannot help that," says the Judge. "It is you, yourself, who is so harsh. Do you imagine that if I continued to judge you as harshly as you do yourself, that you would have survived or had the success in the world and in your own eyes, that you have had? Do you imagine that? You would have long since been destroyed."

"Who then, or what then, continues to judge me in such a demanding, negative, destructive, way?"

"I repeat: it is you, yourself."

These words of the Judge, of the King on the Throne who precedes all being and desire, puzzle me. If I do not experience myself judging myself, then how do I do so? If it is not the Judge, then who is it? If it is not the world rejecting my spirit, then what is it in me? ... Now I see the Orange Tewfik Lady also smiling. I look at one and then the other. I focus upon the one up there in Heaven, the other there in Tewfik Land. Both smile. I know not what to do.

I flee into myself. I feel my own desire now, my own sneaky desire for pleasure and release. The only judge there, the only one to say "sneak" is myself ... All right then, let me imagine that I pleasure myself and see what takes place. These two, the Judge on the Throne and the Orange Tewfik Woman, are benevolent, but now I imagine a further Judge, but this one is out there. It is you, my reader, you who look at these pages. It is you I fear, it is your Judge who can devastate me. And what is it, pray tell, that I think you will say to me? All right. It is this:

"My god, the poor bastard just needs to pleasure himself and he gets all spiritual and excited about it."

Or, good reader, if I do not pleasure myself but rather enjoy your wife instead, then what?

"You bastard! You lying, chicken-shit bastard! Sneak around and play with other men's wives, eh? I'll kill you for that, and with justice!"

Or, good reader, if it is not myself, nor your wife or lover that I pleasure myself with, but you, good woman that you are, loyal wife and true, this is what you say:

"You rotten man! You seducer! Not only do you betray, but you have to let the world know! How rotten you are!"

These are the things you say to me, dear reader, you to whom I address my spiritual insights, you to whom I offer my best — and worst — you whom I serve, bow to, and placate, whose esteem I desire. This is what you say to me. Or so I imagine. But now my own great Judge and my own great Spirit of the Flesh say that they do not feel this. Is it you then, reader? Or is it me? Or is it both of us?

Merely a day later and I am down and defeated, depressed and beaten. After an exhilarating statement and challenge, feeling a deep relation with you, unknown reader, a sense of transcendence, finding a place where rejection is overcome, today I feel down and broken. What is it? Several things perhaps, but the crowning one is another experience of frustration at the hands of my publisher.

Today I called the printer to see if he could find out what his neighbor, the publisher, was doing, if the latter did get the money for the bindery to do its work. I was told that the publisher was not even in his shop. He had gone off to a convention of hair-dressers trying to sell his astrological column! Not even a clue whether the presumed check that was coming to him had cleared the bank! Further, the woman there was mean enough to add that the landlord had been around looking for the rent. Why she had to add that is beyond me. But it is par for where she was earlier in the year — going psychotic, gossiping about the publisher, delaying and making so many errors in the manuscript in preparation for printing.

What can I say? I feel so inarticulate, unable to change anything. I feel that even if these words were to appear that I might be subject to a libel suit, but what I have said is no less than the truth, in terms of horribles done. But where is the me who was riding high a day ago, this person who spoke to you, reader, and told of my fear of judgment and rejection by you and in the speaking, transcending? Where is that I of yesterday? He is still here.

Here I am, trying to tell you of the pain of being the frustrated, defeated, unrecognized, unpublished writer, of the agony of incompetents running the only shop which would even try to bring out my work, of the pain and cruelty and unconsciousness of the people associated with it. Are you there? Do you understand? And who are you? Who are the faces I imagine who are reading this? Not the judges of yesterday.

Rather, I see a young man, an English major in college. He has glasses, is sensitive. I see him compassionate, but cynical, saying, "Well, he can't even express his pain or frustration very well!" And you are right, reader, I can not.

I see a middle-aged psychologist reading this, too. I see you, Madam, also with compassion, saying, "What is this need for recognition and indeed, for punishment, since he seems to get it so much. He must arrange for it somehow."

I raise the same question to myself, lady psychologist. I ask myself, repeatedly, how do I contribute to my victimization? How do I, consciously or unconsciously, abet the very frustrating, painful forces which manage to keep me trapped, rejected, and — the title of this book — a failed, frustrated, unpublished writer!

God doesn't help me, reader! Can you? And if you are reading this, I will have gone beyond this miserable state, will I not? Now though, there is only a dry throat, tight belly, and I am able to neither cry nor rage.

Silenced, thinking of rejections of the past. Reader, is there one among you who will know what I feel? Is there a frustrated writer among you who will know this? Must one be a writer to know this condition of hell or purgatory? But, if it is, why am I here? What crime have I committed? Why am I, like Sisyphus, compelled to push this particular stone up the hill endlessly, bring it to the top and then have it roll to the bottom again? What crime? Hubris? I feel nothing of that.

These pages are like bits of blood from my fingers. I feel every letter I type is a spot of blood from a crippled hand and an inarticulate mouth, all in the poor service of a non-comprehending brain and a near-broken heart. Near-broken. That is interesting. Not yet broken. How much do I need to break it altogether? Total humiliation, I suppose. The book being finally and totally rejected and not coming out at all, with all those who pre-bought copies being stuck. Oh, I can see it: the publisher goes broke — he is very much near there anyway — and too bad. There it is, I am stuck with a thousand printed but unbound copies of my book — if I can get it. I suppose that other creditors would impound everything, even that! Oh no! All those people who ordered after I lectured here and there, all those eighty-plus people stuck. And what shall I say when my friends ask after it? Poor Marvin, again humiliated and foolish.

Can you see it, reader? Can you grasp it, English major, you who may also want to write, have written? Can you empathize with it, psychologist, who is also a person and perhaps has worked as hard as hell in trying to understand herself and her life? I have done these things, too, reader. And what of you who is none of these, just a person looking for entertainment or enlightenment. What do I imagine you saying? "What a bore this man is! Who cares about him or his problems? No wonder he had trouble getting his book out, he is not very interesting!" But, if you are feeling this, you are reading me, too. And if you are, over there in a future state and time, then the hell and purgatory I have been in is at last over and you are looking at my past!

But my past is my present just now. Or rather, what you are seeing, reader, is my horrible present. I can only ask that you try and feel your way into the pain of this abused, frustrated writer and have compassion for him. And do I? Do I have compassion for myself? What was it old Jung said: "At last one finds that the person that needs all one's love is one's self." Yes, it is true. But I need your love, too, reader, there in the future, there in the days when this hell will seem like that I experienced with a tyrannical ship captain with whom I once sailed in the Merchant Marine. I need you, all ten or ten thousand of you, to help redeem this poor, aggrieved, inarticulate, frustrated, unrecognized, even narcissistic writer back here. I need your help out of time and space; I need you to re-create, thus change, this horror. Having said that, I feel a little better. I feel that I can, at least, go on. Perhaps some of your understanding and care, dear reader of the future, has come across time and space and comforted me, enabled me to go on.

Another day, and I have read the foregoing words to my friend L., the only one who seems not only to grasp and connect with what I am saying, but to even bring a higher consciousness to it. She notes, in these pages and these experiences, not only my terrible inarticulateness and, its opposite, a poetic quality, but also that I am never met in the place of my own pain and judgment. The "readers," for example, that I posited in the writing, seem to her to be quite narrow and involved with only right and wrong. Most readers, she thought, would have other reactions, e.g., would be touched by a similar conflict of spirit and flesh and therefore would identify with it or would find me attractive and maybe, would want to "get a piece of me," or would be unable to follow the kind of polarity thinking which I live and with which I struggle. In other words, my own history of self-judgment is hard and unsparing, and it might be easier to have judgment greet me from outside. Further pain, as a matter of fact, comes from the actual judgments in places where I am particularly careful. For example, I am especially sensitive to not treading on the feelings of others, of having a high regard for differences in viewpoint. Despite this, I was judged, once, for having "bad manners."

But now, dear reader of the future, I must return to you and to my friends, and to my situation in Tewfik Land. I must tell you that there was a moment of recovery, of nourishment and care from you, there in the future, to my present and immediate past of yesterday. Your care did indeed enable me to go on from future to present and back again.

I am also aware that all of us here now in Orange Tewfik Land, in the presence of the Lady of the Spirit of the Flesh, are aspects or ways of relating to her and the challenges which she brings: the Tewfik Man, with his sense of strength and self-esteem with which I struggle at this moment; Haggard, in a deeply meditative condition, inward and searching, leading to creative imagination; and the Steersman, amused, volatile, understanding it all, able to be with it and beyond it and away from it — in short, objective; and I, thrown by it into despair, inarticulate, defeated, longing, human.

And I also know that I have not yet been able to achieve even my own self-esteem. Because it is not only the flesh and its longings which thwart me, but it is also the spirit, evasive and hurtful, of that man out there, my publisher!

And now, I am stopped. No words flow from my fingers into and out of this typewriter which stands before me. The utter frustration and impotence, which existed before, is still present. Further, the cold that I "caught" the very evening of my last high point makes me sink further into the flesh. Perhaps the Spirit of the Flesh, the Orange Lady, may be of help here. She alone, perhaps, can help me on my way, just as you, dear reader of the future, sending your understanding and compassion back through time, helped me yesterday.

"Orange Lady of Tewfik," I call out. "Are you there? Are you present to me, even though I sit here, before my typewriter, just out of reach of either Tewfik Land or any of my friends: Haggard, Steersman, or Tewfik Man?"

"I am here, Marvin, mortal and prince, sufferer and noble. You have suffered, it is true, and been ennobled thereby. But I also understand your need to flee from this mortal suffering of the flesh, to be noble among mortals and to be a mortal among the nobles of Tewfik. We of Tewfik Land appreciate this, even if mortals do not. We of Orange Tewfik know this, even if Green Tewfik knew only of what they had to offer you. We, spirits of the flesh, know that you bring the gift of your mortality, your flesh and your suffering, to us. We would recompense you for your devotion by softening that pain and struggle."

"How would you do this, Noble Lady of Tewfik? How would you accomplish this feat, for which I long so desperately?"

"We would, and are doing so, in the very process of our dialogue, mortal man. Are you not aware that this conversation between us is your initiation process, your coming into the Kingship of our Land, the very nobility and authority which you rejected long ago? You are being beaten by the branches as in your dream. Now the beating, however, is administered by the princes of the world, not by us. You have undergone our initiation and now it is the world's turn to provide this. Even as you sit there struggling, the process of the crowning, the making manifest of that which has always existed, will exist, and was not, goes on."

"The Way is the Goal, a master said, I suppose, and I have agreed to that. Lady, Queen of the World of the Flesh-Spirit, what can you now offer to assuage the pain, free the inertia, heal the sickness, inspire the artist?"

"You want a great deal in a moment, Marvin," says the Lady, smiling. "Besides, I am not Queen of this Land, merely a noble among nobles, a princess among princesses. The Queen is yet to appear to you. In that, Haggard was quite right. The Queen, the Muse — whatever you may name her — has not yet permitted herself to appear to you. It is, just as you surmised, first necessary to initiate yourself inwardly and outwardly. Now then, what about your self-esteem?"

"What about it?"

"Do you have it, like the shining, radiant, Tewfik Man? Do you not know him as part of your Self? Do you not guess or realize, that just as the Knight, a Tewfik in his own right, came to you long ago in the childhood of your present life, in the dream of your middle twenties, and in the creative writing of the man of 40, that the other "Knight" of that great dream was the Tewfik Man, himself? Did they not both beat you in that dream? And is it not true that your beating with the Trees of Life was not very difficult at all?"

"Yes, I remember that dream, and I recall with fondness and appreciation my friend the Knight and his son, whose stories I have written."

"The 'beating' of these Knights was not painful for you. These Knights of adventure and creation have arisen from within. Your greater pains have been from without, from the world and the border region, the world of matter."

"Yes, Madam, you speak the truth as I understand it."

"So then, mortal and prince, it is up to us of Tewfik Land, particularly of Orange Tewfik, to aid you on your way."

"Yes, great lady, but how? How will you help me in these questions of flesh and matter?"

I see her now smiling. Her light skin, very slightly orange, her orange-red lips, her brown eyes and orange-red, fall-leaf colored hair enchant me. She smiles.

"Take me in, Marvin," she says, whispering.

"And how, fair lady?" I ask.

"Hold me," she says.

I hold her. I sense her smell, delicate; I feel her flesh, warm and tender; I smell her breath, clear and light. I realize that I can only gradually sense her substantiality, I can only slowly feel her reality as concretely as this typewriter, that world outside my window ... I cough. I feel heavy, feel my bowels stir — in short, I feel the opposite of this lovely, delicate lady. I feel the sickness, torpor, and excreta of the body and not its beauty, attraction, joy.

"Come closer," says the Lady.

I do. But the torpor and dis-ease and excreta press harder upon me. I feel pain and sickness, the foulness of body, and not its joy.

"Closer yet," she says. And I cough once more, even louder. I feel even sicker and even more absorbed by headache and excreta. I would excrete this illness, torpor and poison.

"Then excrete it," says the Lady.

Now I belch and some poison air is excreted.

We both laugh, the Lady Princess of the Spirit of Flesh and I. The belch did it. And I excrete further.

"Is that all, Lady?" I say, as I return from that ordinary task and activity that all humans perform, and that which makes us less than gods. "Is that all this is about?"

"Don't be as narrow as those judges you see out there, Marvin," she replies. "That isn't all. Not by half. There is urination, too!"

Once more she laughs and I do too. Getting rid of the poisons, of the illness, of the dregs; it is as ordinary and natural as that. But now my neck aches and I feel the pain of old wounds; of pains in neck and back, which do not respond so easily as the ordinary, daily eliminations which are no pain at all, except when hindered.

"Except when hindered," she repeats with emphasis. I realize that she is speaking of the muscular tension that builds during an entire life as a result of hurts, fears, withheld rages, and anxieties.

Now I cough again, but less in pain and more in relief, as I begin to feel a little better. Just as I did when I felt compassion and understanding from across time and space. Now I feel the acceptance of the smaller pain, the aching and torpor of this cold or flu, and I do not struggle so.

"Do not struggle so," repeats the Lady, with a smile. Her parroting of my statements makes them heavier, suggesting significance. Do not struggle so. Yes. "I am, dear Lady, eager to change my identity from Struggler and Victim, to Creative, Happy, or Serene One. You reinforce, 'do not struggle so.' Let it flow" ... Now I sigh and breathe more easily, become aware that my breathing was shallow in my struggle. My body relaxes more and I feel the illness less.

"That is Tewfik," smiles the Lady.

"Yes," say I, and I feel the sense of a crown being put on my head. It is a small, thin crown, made of a gold which is both yellow and orange, the yellow which I brought to Tewfik Land, and the orange of the Tewfik Woman. But this gold crown has on it green jewels, flashing and bright, from the Tewfik Man. There is a hint of other jewels on that crown, red and blue ones as well. The crowning is taking place and is real, but not so whole, so concrete, as one might wish. It is as real as is the Lady of Tewfik right now. The Crown is unfinished because it is equally real and unreal, just as I am equally real and unreal at this moment. And even as you, dear reader, of both present and future are much in my sight and utterly foreign to my blind eyes.

"And of self-esteem?" asks the Tewfik Lady.

"Enough to survive, dear Lady," say I, "each moment."

Now I see the Green Tewfik Man smiling. He stands with arms enfolded upon his chest, radiating intense green light, nodding his head. He — and I — share a certain self-esteem.

After a day, I resolved to get some legal help *vis-à-vis* my publisher, advice about my contract and see if something could not be done in the matter. That felt better. A friend suggested that when taking a stand, as I do against the negative Mercurius, that I might also invoke, in magical fashion, Thoth, the Mercury of

Egypt. Thoth, after all, is himself the patron of magic and is indeed the God-form that I am dealing with generally. Why not call upon him according to the ancient prayer?

Let me then invoke the God-form Thoth, also called Tahuti, just as the ancient prayer has it:

> "O Thou Majesty of the Godhead, Wisdom-Crowned Tahuti, Lord of the Gates of the Universe, Thee, Thee I invoke!
>
> "O Thou whose head is an Ibis, Thee, Thee I invoke!
>
> "Thou who holdest in Thy right hand the magic wand of Double Power, and who bearest in the left hand the Rose and Cross of Light and Life, Thee, Thee I invoke!
>
> "Thou whose head is as an Emerald, and whose Nemyss is as the night-sky blue, Thee, Thee I invoke!
>
> "Thou whose skin is of flaming orange as though it burned in a furnace: Thee, Thee, do I invoke!
>
> "Behold! I am yesterday, today, and the brother of tomorrow! I am born again and again. Mine is the unseen force wherefrom the Gods are sprung, which giveth life unto the dwellers in the Watchtowers of the Universe.
>
> "I am the charioteer in the East, Lord of the Past and of the Future, who seeth by his own inward light. I am the Lord of Resurrection, who cometh forth from the dusk, and whose birth is from the House of Death. O ye two divine hawks upon your pinnacles, who keep watch over the Universe! Ye who accompany the bier unto the House of Rest, who pilot the Ship of Ra, ever advancing to the height of heaven! Lord of the Shrine which standeth in the center of the Earth!
>
> "Behold! He is in me, and I in Him! Mine is the radiance wherein Ptah floateth over his firmament. I travel upon high! I tread upon the firmament of Nu! I raise a flashing flame with the lightning of mine eye, ever rushing onward in the splendour of the daily glorified Ra, giving life to the dwellers on Earth. If I say, 'Come up upon the mountains,' the celestial waters shall flow at my word. For I am Ra, incarnate; Kephra, created in the flesh! I am the eidolon of my Father, Lord of the City of the Sun.
>
> "The God who commands is in my mouth. The God of Wisdom is in my heart. My tongue is the sanctuary of Truth, and a God sitteth upon my lips. My word is accomplished every day, and the desire of my heart realizes itself like that of Ptah when he created his

works. Since I am eternal, everything acts according to my designs, and everything obeys my words.

"Therefore do Thou come forth unto me, from Thine abode in the Silence; Unutterable Wisdom, All-Light, All-Power.

"Thoth, Hermes, Mercury, Odin; by whatever name I call Thee, Thou art still un-Named and Nameless for Eternity. Come Thou forth I say, and aid and guard me in this work of Art.

"Thou Star of the East that didst conduct the Magi: Thou art the same, all present in Heaven and in Hell. Thou that vibratest between the Light and the Darkness, rising, descending, changing forever, yet ever the same; The Sun is Thy Father! Thy Mother, the Moon! The Wind hath borne Thee in its bosom, and earth hath ever nourished the changeless Godhead of Thy Youth.

"Come Thou forth I say, Come Thou forth, and make all spirits subject unto me! So that every spirit of the firmament and of the Ether; upon the Earth and under the Earth; on Dry Land, and in the Water, of Whirling Air and of Rushing Fire, and every spell and scourge of God, may be obedient unto me!"

That is the end of the prayer invoking the great God, Thoth, the Mercury and Hermes of Egypt, and the Tahuti who is the great patron of Magic. I stare at his Egyptian form, seated in profile, with his human body and Ibis head. On that head is a strange crown with two hawks. He holds a double-wand and rose-cross with great dignity. He is described, in the prayer, as colored in deep orange and I wonder if he is connected with the Lady of Orange-Tewfik Land.

"Of course he is, Marvin," I hear from the Lady, who seems to be present even though I do not see her. "I am here, Marvin, summoned or not, as your wise man said. I am here, as I said to you before, to help you. We will persist until other assistance arrives. Yes, I said this Thoth is of us, this Tahuti is of us, just as he is with you in a different form. Do you not call him Steersman or Trickster? Is he not there with you and your friend, Haggard? Did you not even call him this, many a time?"

"Yes, great Lady, we have done so. But now we seem to need him or greet him in another form, another kind of magic. This is not the magic of ever-changing shapes and images, a potpourri of fantasy which leads to art. This magic which we need is the magic of indirect effect, of accomplishing something in that material world out there, where I am so ineffective; of having my will be done in a way which eludes me; of working my desire in such a way that the fantasy-words-images of the self-same Mercurius who is with us, will effect and change the dark Mercurius who hinders us out there, in the form of the publisher. Behind him, no doubt, are all those other hinderers of this world."

"I know, Marvin," she says sadly. And now she is quiet, but I feel her commiseration, concern, and care.

I turn now to the picture and image of the great Thoth and Tahuti. I am moved to say my prayer to him, not only in the words already given in tradition, but in other ones.

> "O Thou Tahuti, Lord of Magic; hear me! I have said the prayer to you as of old, but I would add my own painful, human words to invoke you. I have known you, Lord, as Mercurius, as Hermes, as guide of my soul, as leader and changer, and in the many ways of the life of the spirit, in a bottle and out of it, as containing you and contained by you. I know you, Lord, but not as you are here, in that alien Egyptian form. I do not know you so. Perhaps it is just because I have not known you in that form — from the land where spirit and flesh were so close as to be synonymous — that I have suffered so. Perhaps it is just this ignorance, Lord, not knowing how to bring my own spirit into the concrete reality of this world, that has put me on bad terms with you. If so, O Lord, if I have offended you, please forgive it. If I have not honored you in the right manner, please instruct me. And if I should, as the invocation says, not merely call upon you, but even let your form take me over and for me to become you, then all right, do that too. Speak to me, Lord, and let me hear your name and your ..."

The Ibis takes on life but stays in one place. There is no word, but there is some movement. He lifts his wand and shakes his Ankh, his Tree which combines the rose and the cross. He nods once and nods once again. The hawks upon his crown also nod in their opposite directions. I understand that the great Lord Tahuti, the Great Thoth, has heard me and acknowledged me. My desire is known to him, my wish is clear.

I feel now a calling to come into him, to let the form evoke itself from within me, in sensation and in feeling, in the flesh. I shiver, and suddenly feel like a bird. I cough and feel a little foolish. But now the Orange Tewfik Lady calms me, as if I am, indeed, a flighty bird, sensitive and nervous. I hold the wand in my hand, face it toward the world. I hold it firmly.

"My will be done," I think. "Let my words go forth in peace and success. Let the hinderer hinder no more. Let him go in peace, if he wills, provided he joins in the effort, and let him languish in sorrow if he does not. Let it be."

These thoughts come to me, as I hold the wand, and I feel powerful, in the grip of the Throne of the Most High Thoth and Tahuti. They do seem like other forms of the King and Mercurius, the Judge and the Steersman, but I feel them in a different way. I feel them now in the Orange way, with flesh and substance, and not in my own old blue and yellow manner, as spirit and intuition, as thought and insight. I have known him, in the past, as "Charioteer" (in my book, *The Quest,* sequel to *The Tree),* and as the Steersman, but now I feel substance. Now I hold the Ankh, the cross and rose which is indeed the Tree of Life. Is this not the name of my own still-unpublished book? Is this not, great Lord (now I turn to Him, instead of being him), a work in Your Name, and in Your Service? Why then should there be hindering? Pray, tell me."

I watch the hand of the Lord and the arm. It is strange to see that Ibis head move that human arm. The arm gestures and the cross shakes. Now, just as the Wand was pointed toward the World, the cross is pointed toward me. I begin to feel that cross, that Tree of Life, inside me, just as I had learned in my long, long work with the Knight and the Son of the Knight and the Grandson, too. I understand that the power of the Tree is internal: to evoke, to live, to experience, to fulfill. I also understand that the power of the wand, held in the right hand, is to make one's work known, to fulfill that Tree in the world. Tahuti, Master of Magic, is the master of both. The hawks upon his crown serve both; they look forward and back, outside and within; the vision is past and future, outer and inner. The effect is also dual: wand for outer effect, tree for inner. The God functions that way.

"I thank you, Lord, for this insight and realization," I say. "I am fully aware that the wand has not been well handled by me. I am painfully aware that I have not done well in its use. Can you instruct me?"

There is a silent nod from the Ibis. But there is also an unspoken statement from him, to the effect, "not yet." More must be known by me, more fulfilled and initiated, before I become master of the Wand of Double Power.

But, I wonder, will my own little *Tree* appear? Will there be sufficient "effect" right now, after this work, this prayer and invocation, to result in that which is desired? The answer seems to be "yes." The Ibis nods, and I sense that I must ask no more.

I turn then to the Orange Tewfik Lady and hold her. I feel her substantiality, her reality. I sense the Orangeness of her, and I wonder if, indeed ...

"I know what you wonder," says Orange Tewfik Lady. "I know." "Let the spirit work its way. We of Orange Tewfik know this spirit. Can you not feel the Orangeness? Can you not sense the subtle power in it?"

"I can, fair Lady, more than before."

"Then trust and follow. And let it be for now. You have prayed, invoked, dialogued, and acted; now let it, us, act."

I accept her suggestion and withdraw.

Another day has passed, and I am still in the grip of sadness about my book, *The Tree*. Being the "Unpublished Writer" nags at me. Even though I have prayed and invoked, plus spoken with the lawyer, I am down and defeated. The reality of the waiting and frustration is almost too much for me. As if to make it worse, people come to me who have had books published, or are about to! The entire matter eludes my understanding and my sense of order.

"Orange Lady of Tewfik, I call to you! You were kind enough to have compassion for me, to assure me. Was this merely a pablum to assuage a hungry child, or was it the truth? And, if it is the truth, what is the meaning of this? Was it like that dream I had of the Knight, when I resigned from my Jungian Society? The Knight told me that he no longer had a cause to serve. And then I dreamed that I gave up a five dollar bill and a one dollar bill into the blue. I received back six silver dimes. I understood that, at the time, to mean that I was to sacrifice the values (coins) of the natural man (five) and egotism (one), and receive the creative energies connected with the feminine and totality (six silver dimes). Later on that year, after I began to write the story of *The Tree,* I consciously used a pattern of six times ten — six parts for each story, ten stories. But I wonder if the five plus one is not even more concrete. I had to advance five thousand dollars to the publisher to help bring it out, and now there remains a need of one thousand dollars in order to get the binding finished on the first thousand copies. Is it as concrete as that? Please answer, Tewfik Woman, or help me to get a better answer from Thoth or Tahuti, with whom I spoke yesterday."

"Your wishes are granted, Marvin," says Orange Tewfik Woman. "It merely takes time to bring them about. Nothing more need be done by you, except as you have set out. I am not the possessor of the information that you desire, with regard to money, amounts and dates; nor do I know any that are. I do know, and we of Tewfik know, that the work is already done, the honor given, performed and accomplished. The problem of time, of the materialization of the work beyond Tewfik Land is a difficult one, but have no fear."

"I thank you for your support and assurances, dear Lady, as I have already been supported by my friend Haggard, by the Steersman, by Mercurius, and Thoth Himself. But still, it seems so hard. For even writing here seems just illusion. So much illusion. Hope, belief, desire, trust, work, and then illusion. Hence the failed writer, unpublished artist. Perhaps these words themselves need to be known. Perhaps, sometime, another suffering writer, himself rejected, frustrated, unhappy, may read these words and in the reading, knowing that the book he is reading has, of course, been published, will take heart. Take heart then, writer, future reader of these words; here at last, is someone who has suffered like you, but has been fulfilled.

"I think now, Tewfik Lady, of Henry Miller, and his words to me. He called me a fine writer and gifted, but he felt he could not help me to get published. He told me the story of the little boy who tried to help the butterfly out of the chrysalis, only to cause his death. That of course, indicated that the spirit requires its own work and time, else it be destroyed. I understood what he meant. And perhaps it is true. I suspect that if ever I am a realized writer, that I shall not like having writers hounding me to get their work published! But still, there could be some little help, could there not? Does the divine plan require that I not get help, concretely? Then I think of the musical play, "Fiddler on the Roof," where a poor Jew, Tevye, sings a song, wishing to be a rich man and asking God's help. Would it harm the divine plan, he implores? But then, he does not succeed either, does he? Will I? Will I see my work, finally, in print? So close now. It sits there on my desk, a book without a binding. What a symbol: a book without a binding!

"It seems to me, Tewfik Lady, to reflect my own skinless, or thin-skinned relation to the cruel forces outside and within. But now, at least, the Judges are not as cruel and demeaning from within as they used to be. Indeed, even the great Judge is not harsh, saying that I am hard on myself! The gods reassure me!

"And yet ... When I was a youth and received lavish praise, I blushed and tended to deny it. Just as in the dream of the crowning, rejecting the honors. Now as a middle-aged man I see rewards that I think are due me, and they are denied! Paradox, a life of paradox!

"Is this what you mean, Lady of Tewfik? Is this the painful struggle to really accept the Crown of Tewfik? To undergo all this doubt and rejection? If so, then what about my rejection of the victim role, of no longer being identified with Jesus on the Cross? Now it seems to me that this powerful and divine image is hardly more than a symbol of man suffering his own muscular tension!"

"Marvin," says the Tewfik Woman. "You think, you try to understand, but you do not accept. You did not accept the honors then and you do not accept defeat now! But this is how you are and were and, no doubt, shall be. As perverse and difficult as the very Mercurius and dark Thoth that you both serve and battle! Do you not see that the whole process has been your goal? Do you not see that you are closer to your goal of wholeness and oneness than ever? Even in your failure and despair, you are closer to joy, to acceptance. Did you not, a few days ago, feel a piece of the crowning taking place within you? ... Look now at the crown. Some black stones are there as well as the green. They are like black teardrops, with a shining white light within. Obsidian perhaps, like the dark stone of the Self. These dark sufferings are to be worn as jewels in your Crown as well!"

"I do not wish to wear this suffering like a jewel. I do not want to be pitied. I do not feel that I can even express it adequately. At least I can't do it any better than I have already. I want to move away from this pit of pain, this place of frustration, to the Crown of joy."

"And you shall. Only wait and be patient."

"And what more can I do?"

"No more. It is done, shall be done. It is true that you have waited long and in model patience. Wait a bit more."

"I shall wait. I have no choice ... But comfort me, Lady Tewfik. Have compassion for this stuffy-nosed, trembling, perplexed, defeated, middle-aged man!"

A few days later, in the midst of continuing pain and frustration about the book, along with body pain, I dream:

> I am at a large marketplace: worldly, busy. I see D, the publisher, behind a counter. He seems to be selling drugs and such. He is embarrassed to see me, mumbles something about not having the money, just as he did in waking life. Then I see a second D, who is serious, firm, hard. The latter D is the Judge. I see that Judge and Mercurius are two forms of the same thing, that here they are both negative in the shape of D. Great suffering is felt by me in this dream: despair, futility, frustration, humiliation. How can this negativity be overcome? I ask myself this as I awaken.

I thought about the dream afterwards: if they are one, the two D's, Mercurius and Judge, why do they not operate in the actual man? I sense these two in myself, with Mercurius as flow, mostly positive, but negative in uncontainable desire. The Judge was *at* me before, but is no longer. I have the Judge now in my own ego. But what does it mean that D is both? Mercurius as the trickster in him and the judge in him as limitation of his desires?

Yes, now I can see it! Now I see and pity him, his suffering in body, too — worse than mine. He has heart trouble, I have neck and low back pain. His feeling function is poor. My tenacity (neck) and sex-hunger drive (low back) are troublesome. But I am his victim as well as my own. He is a victim, too, perhaps? Yes, I think so. I can see it. He is several years older than I and even more of a failure. His marriages failed and his relation with his children failed, too, as he related his story to me, whereas mine are positive, mostly, supporting, and full of love. My wife and children are the last unfailed parts of my life, really. So I can have pity for him too. But I hate to be his victim, even if he does not intend it and can not help it. I would have appreciated honesty and some feeling-connection on his part. So before I was a victim of the Judge, outside and inside; now I am a victim of Mercurius, outside and inside!

The dream shows me that D, like me, has Judge and Mercurius, senex-Saturn and puer-Mercurius in him also. All right. Now, in the morning, after the hopelessness and agony of the small hours, I can see and recover a little.

But what do you want of me? What is it, Lord? You know what I want of you. Why such suffering? ... Not just me, you say, but D also. And he is just as important in the scheme of things as I am? I suppose so; of course. But what of my prayer, to you as Thoth, and your positive response thereto? What of that? ... Still true, you say? Despite my despair, despite my having practically given up? ... Yes, you say, silently. I am still chosen, and it will be as I wish. But first look at D, a man like myself. A writer like myself, broken, failed, struggling, and with ambition even greater than mine. Illusion? Self-deception? Like mine?

Now I see Haggard looking at me kindly, and the Orange Tewfik Woman is almost in tears for me. I think about the sad Japanese movie that I saw last night, "Twenty-Four Eyes." That had real tragedy in it — war, death of a husband and of a child, broken lives of her pupils, death of most of them, blindness to one of the two remaining of the original beautiful, happy group. All this tragedy happens to a dedicated, beautiful teacher. My life is easy in comparison. Hers was a "three handkerchief story," as the Japanese say. Mine, I am both glad and afraid to say, is merely a "one handkerchief" tale. But it is mine, anyway, Lord, and sad to me! ... Haggard, I am glad to have you as a friend! And Tewfik Lady, your tears and gentleness make up for the lack of these fine qualities in Mercurius ...

Now I see that Steersman smiling at me, too. But he is Mercurius, after all. I know your benevolence, Angel! Green Tewfik Man stands and smiles, friendly also. I am not abandoned nor utterly deceived. And I have seen, in my dream, that D, even

D, is Judge and Mercurius and suffering also. So even I can have compassion for him, even if I am his victim! Does the Judge and Mercurius beyond D need my feeling or that of the Tewfik Woman? I do not know right now. I am glad to have my own!

And now, having rediscovered compassion and objectivity, I dream again. In this dream there is a book which I see, a critical history of modern art, particularly concerned with writing. It is largely a history of decadence. The author is bright, talented, and starts with the thesis that someone named Boileau or Baudoin is the beginning of it all. He continues on in his book with surrealists, expressionists, symbolists, etc., and includes Henry Miller, D.H. Lawrence, and others as well. Some of the writers are good, he shows, and some are really very decadent. It has the smell of the putrid in it. Again I awaken in despair.

Is this, I think, a further indication of illusion for me? Should I attempt to fulfill this book of the unknown "critic"? And what of the putrid? Why do I not receive support in my dream, but am compelled to seek it, work it out for myself, as I did with the previous dream? But now I see that this is a statement-type of dream. It is an objective statement of what exists in the outer world. It neither supports me nor criticizes me, merely reports. I need not take this personally at this point perhaps. It merely shows what is what. But what of Boileau or Baudoin? Who are they? Monsieur Boileau comes to mind, of Charlie Chaplin's film of modern decadence as one, a true trickster, and dark; and then that French writer that Henry Miller liked so well, what was his name? Something like that. But no matter. It is simply a statement of what is. Where I fit in all this, I can not say.

Another day, and I have spoken to my lawyer. He has given me no great hope about the contract I have signed, which gives all the power and money to the publisher, little to me. The best that can be done, perhaps, is to persuade him to sign a new contract which would give me more of a share, more control, and free me from the obligation to do a second book with him. The only thing that might induce him to do this would be self-interest, such as advance more money, the $1000 of the dream, perhaps, and thus pay for the binding of those books already available. Should D be willing to reduce his profits and control to a reasonable place, then this would be fine with me. Yet he never answers the telephone, it is already disconnected. Perhaps he will respond to his own great need. He has little invested in the book, though, and has already collected on the pre-payment of eighty of them.

Well, I called the typesetter lady next door to him and she agreed to leave him a note, asking him to call me since I had a proposition for him. Perhaps he will call this weekend. I hope that we — the lawyer, D, and I — can meet and work it out amicably and fairly. Fairness, I think, has long since jumped out the window for me, I am afraid. In my foolishness and fear, I signed a contract which was adverse for me. I can only hope that he is not merely manipulative and has some sense of decency as well. Better not hope for that; better to relate primarily to his sense of gain.

My God! I seem to learn so slowly about the world, and about people's needs for self and self alone. Screw the other guy! But I can't do that, or won't. This is because my own self esteem would be damaged. No, not so. If I could get away with it now, I think I would try to "screw" D, as they say, as much as possible, without compunction, since he has done so to me. Dog eat dog, and all those other horrible homilies.

"Oh, Orange Tewfik Lady, Green Tewfik Man, Haggard and Steersman, my friends! I seem to be so vulnerable and stupid in this world, where support for one's spirit is rare."

"That is a rare quality, indeed." It is Haggard speaking. "Rare." He nods, but says nothing more.

I turn to the Orange Tewfik Woman. She is sad and then smiles sweetly. She knows what I am saying. She knows about the publisher and about my friend from Switzerland who cannot understand my spirit nor connect with it. She understands and knows. She suffers with me in it also. She knows. She also knows that it will be all right.

"Is it illusion, my friends?" I say. "Here I am with you, feeling your love, support, and understanding as well as your predictive statement that 'it will be all right.' But can not that be illusion, too? Are you, perhaps, figments of my imagination, created by me or my need to hear the things that you say to me? Are you ..."

"I am no figment," says the Steersman, "and I am not so totally supportive of you, as you already know."

"Nor am I," says Green Tewfik.

"And, of course, I am surely not," says Haggard.

"But I am!" says Orange Tewfik Lady.

"You are?" ask I, a little surprised and puzzled.

"Yes!" she responds. "I am and shall be whatever you wish me to be. You desire a figment, I shall be it. You desire me to be real, I shall be it. Whatever you wish."

"That throws me," say I. "I do not know what to do with that. If you are a figment, then ... but, if I created you and now you have your own life and with that are willing to do whatever I wish, then you have your own reality!"

"Of course."

"I suppose I knew that before. But really I wish to know if your positive predictions will be borne out."

"Do you want them to?"

"Of course!"

"Then it shall be!"

I am at a loss now on how to proceed. I seem to be in a solipsism and yet to not be in it. "Gentlemen! Tewfik Woman agrees to be a figment or whatever I wish, including the possibility that I merely created her. You do not."

"If I am not a figment," says Green Tewfik, "then neither is she, since we both come from Tewfik Land, and I am surely not created by you."

"But why does she say this?" ask I.

"What else could she say to help you get out of your pain and dilemma? To assert her reality, as we have done, would resolve nothing. To agree with you would be false and also solves nothing. So she responds as she responds, which is to stop this futile line of questioning. What is needed here, I think, as she said to you earlier, is faith. 'Trust,' she said, I believe. Trust her. Can you trust us, too?"

"Faith," I say. "I don't know. That is hard for me; particularly in connection with writing and books. But I can wait, patiently, working, going day by day, step by step. The faith that I can embrace is a devotion to this process. A faith that the process leads somewhere. That I still have."

"Enough then," says Tewfik Man.

"I love you," says Tewfik Woman, embracing me.

I have just returned from a meeting with the publisher and my lawyer. My lawyer believes that the publisher is close to bankruptcy. He is trying to get a new contract signed which will give ownership of the book to me. If the man does give up the ghost in his forthcoming heart surgery or goes broke, then I will at least have the plates in hand.

I can not really describe the meeting. I can only state that once again I am torn between illusion and reality, but which is which? I can not write, can not report, can not say anything. The failed writer continues to be a failure, both in the sense of getting his words into the world, and in expressing the "facts" now. My God, the facts, the function of sensation, reality, grasping the outer world, seems not only to elude me, but to defeat me endlessly. And now the scenario has not only a mercurial entrepreneur, but a lawyer too. A realistic person is now working on my behalf, but what happens to my vision and its expression? The play goes on.

"My friends: Steersman, Tewfik Man and Woman, Haggard, are you there?"

"We are," they all answer.

"Yes, you are, I know. Yet I am alone with my illusion. You can not help me, and I can not help you. I do not know which is which. There is a certain degree of demoralization in me right now. My fingers can hardly type. I feel the pain in my back, another radiates down my left arm. I think of the illusions and pain of my friend, H, too. Give up, I say to myself. Give up. But to whom and to what? Where is there a reality, an eye in the storm of confusion wherein there is some certainty? There is none. Haggard, let me ask you. Can you offer me any advice, thought, or feeling in this?"

I see him looking sad and nodding. He speaks. "It is as I have said. It will be well. Part of the process, the procedure. More than that, time and place, I can not say. I can only say that you have my sympathy and understanding."

The others nod. They, too, have no more to say, except that to still believe, have hope, nay, have certainty. I have no more to say either.

Yesterday, at the meeting with the publisher, after he called and said that there was no money forthcoming for the binding of the book, and after my lawyer expressed the belief that the man was already essentially bankrupt, that many of his promises, if not all of them, were pure wind, yesterday, as I say, I was near bottom. I felt totally possessed by illusion, dazzled by the publisher's promises and words, and even by my own inner friends and voices: Steersman, the Man and Woman of Tewfik, and Haggard. I felt total beguilement.

So, a day of despair and illusion. The night was not much better. I could not capture my dream, but it had to do with the sense of illusion. Even hope, I felt, was illusion. Yesterday to cap my not being aware, I inadvertently drove my car into the rear end of another car. Not much damage, but more discomfort and failure. Yes, I thought, the world is collapsing, children and orphans look for homes as they flee the Southeast Asia wars. So much pain and viciousness in the world; my own plight is small in comparison. But there is no comparison, I thought. I live my life, carry my load and obligations, but still this isolation and aloneness with illusion is its own agony and not diminished by the greater agonies of others, however total, physical and complete they are. I do not compare, I only note and struggle with my own.

I awakened in a somewhat better frame of mind: less body pain, less sense of ridiculousness and humiliation. More acceptance of the process, just as my inner friends had said.

Just an hour or so ago, the publisher called me — called me, mind you, in itself a fantastic thing, since I have had enormous difficulty in even reaching him over the months! He informed me of good news. The money he expected from the east will be forthcoming; enough of it, even, to bind the entire first thousand books, not only the three hundred already ordered. The bindery, he said, has already started work. He expects to have his check in a day or two and the work should be completed before his heart surgery in a week!

Almost too good to be true! Can one believe it? More illusion? But no, he said, we shall meet at his office in one week, sign the new contract and, hopefully, there will be books to send out to all those who ordered it. An end to humiliation? A true beginning of the "success"? But even now I am not sure. I tell my wife the good news and she, too, is suspicious. Did he round up the money because of fear of the lawyer? Is the money really at the bindery? Phone up and see. ... I try to find the number, but can not. I phone the printer to get it, but he refuses to give me the number. He says he will find it out himself and let me know if I call back tomorrow. O.K., but I hope that D will not be angry at my checking up on him.

How the worm turns! Now I am afraid of his anger! But I do trust and feel that the work will be coming out, just as my inner friends believed and promised. But I also feel strange. I am fearful and uncertain, not as elated as I thought I would be. Perhaps elation will appear when I hold the true book in my hands! I am certain it will be so. So many disappointments finally make one a little careful, I suppose. I have gone up and down with this publisher's promises so many times that it is right to be wary.

"But, inner friends, are you there? What do you feel?"

Steersman smiles and nods. I see Tewfik Woman, her skin milky orange, lips bright, eyes closed. She too seems happy. Haggard smiles as does the Green Tewfik Man. They are pleased, as am I. But this fear and uncertainty lingers.

I am feeling alone, here in my office on a Friday and empty. There is a hunger in my belly. I am fearful of writing, feeling empty. Yesterday, I was full of the sense of illusion, since it seemed that my whole book work and publishing was going to collapse; the writer was, indeed, an illusory business. I concluded that I would have to arrive at the sense of writing for itself alone, rather than having a sense of mission, being a carrier of the

Crown or anything else. I felt fear in being alone with the emptiness, of not being a writer at all, only possessed by illusion. But then the publisher called and once again there is hope for the book to be out. I had a feeling of well-being yesterday afternoon, yet also emptiness in my belly, and a fear of this well-being as more illusion and even afraid of being alone.

I remembered that there was one time in my life when I feared being alone, only one. Normally, being alone is a pleasurable thing for me: dreamy, contented, active, alive, tormented, planning, thoughtful, cosmic, anything but fear-inspiring. But that one time — I must have been about four — I was with my mother at a resort. I awakened in the night and called out to her, but she was not there. I felt an immediate panic and then a realization that there was music going on and that she was in the main hotel, only a hundred yards away from our cottage, and that she was dancing probably. I grew a little calmer but then remembered that she had promised not to leave me that night. She did so anyway. I can understand that now, of course: her need to be entertained, to dance, to have fun, and the lack or even necessity of a sitter. My God, the poor thing was only twenty three or twenty-four! But then, I remember, I was very frightened. I called out and was afraid of the unknown things in the dark. I remember it powerfully now.

To whom do I address myself now? It seems to be that unknown reader of the distant future who will be seeing this. I seem to be again the Writer addressing his Public. All right, then, Reader of the Writer, what are you thinking?

"I think, friend Writer," I imagine you, future reader, to be saying to me, "I think that you worry too much about whether you are a writer. Those are merely technical matters, appropriate to the craft of a writer and not, I think, of great interest to one such as myself, who cares more about a story, a point, a feeling, an experience, than technique."

"You are right, friend Reader," say I. "I shall have to work this out myself some time and not burden you with it."

And now, I am feeling increasingly weird. Hungry for something, alone, a feeling in my belly which defies description. Stimuli to take me away from this strange feeling of aloneness and emptiness? Cars drive by rapidly outside, the phone is at hand, but I am alone. The weird feeling seems to be associated with that childhood time when I called out for help. It was then, perhaps, that the thought came, "You are chosen and special, just as you were told and felt when you were three, but now you are four, and you must realize that this specialness does not bring with it the sense of being loved. God is like mother, not quite there for you when you want her."

That is the thought that comes to this Unpublished Writer, as he contemplates the hunger in his belly. This is consistent with that first experience at three and with this later one at four. To extrapolate, for that boy it would seem that God, the Sun, is gone in the dark. In the darkness of night, there is no love from God, and mother is quite unreliable. Yes, clear enough.

But the belly pain lingers, a sort of hunger. It seems like a hungry ghost, a wisp of something which makes me shiver, then yawn, and shiver again. It is a body feeling, not to be fully worded, a meat of response which can not be breaded with the words to prepare it for the cooking fires of literary consciousness.

... The printer just called and told me that the bindery has not started yet, since the publisher has not, in fact, given them the money! D has not yet received the money he spoke about. The meeting is scheduled for next week, his surgery just after. If the money does not come in time, what of the bindery? Another three week wait? God! Horrible!

A sense of meaninglessness. A sense that if the boy is not a hero, he is nothing. If mother does not come, he is nothing. If mother does not love him, he is nothing. And, if God does the same, it is even worse. Mother is like God, or the reverse. God chooses him as special, tells him so, expects great things of him, and abandons him. The same is true of mother. Mother thinks he is oh so smart, so kind, but is very critical of him, too, and abandons him. That's how it is.

Well then, is life like that? You work hard, you think you are special, you hope for the reward, the "recognition," and being "heard," but you are not. But meaninglessness comes. If Mother does not come when you need her, then all her professed love is nothing. If God does not bring you recognition, then all his professed chosenness is nothing.

Several days have passed since the last entry. By now it becomes more and more apparent that the publisher is a fraud. He lies totally. I managed to call the bindery and was told that at no time did the publisher speak of providing money for binding as he had told me. Further, the bindery said that they expect six hundred dollars from me for the binding, that the total cost of binding a thousand copies was $750, not the $1000+ that the publisher had said, nor the $600 for three hundred copies. So, total lies. Today, I go over the new possible contract with my lawyer and tomorrow will be the day of confrontation with the publisher. Such agonies of the last days: fear, humiliation, foolishness.

But, at the same time, I sense my deepening connection with a non-verbal level, with the energy of union which is not giving-receiving, but sharing. Hard to describe, but I sense the need to move from a psychology of struggle, of integration by inclusion, stimulation, conflict, activity, to one of integration by means of what feels best at the moment. The latter is not to deny one's responsibilities, duties, etc., but to enjoy those moments, not so designated as requirements of living, by listening to the needs of one's total system at that moment, the body-psyche speaking. This leads to the writing: the need to write out of pleasure, for itself, and not out of need for fame, publication, or even to be in the mode of active imagination. I don't know if I can do this. I am wondering what the Tewfik Lady, representative of the body-psyche, spirit of the flesh, says about this. I am trying to listen to my own energy flow and still attend to a dialogue with her, an image of connection.

"Are you there, Tewfik Woman? And do you know what has transpired with me these days?"

"I know."

Now there is silence, while I again reflect upon the senseless-ness of this act, the delusion contained therein, since I still hope to be writing for a public that exists out there. Why am I writing? To report? For continuity? Yes.

"But I want that connection, that body-psyche place with you, Tewfik Woman."

"And you may have it."

"How, pray tell?"

"By just being here now with me." She touches me ... There is a phone interruption. I am disjointed, trying ...

"Lady, I should be still."

"Should be still," she echoes, looks sad and weeps.

Our relation is disrupted.

"Woman of Tewfik, I love you. I love you in your silence, your care for me. I love your listening in this wordless way. I deeply feel that care, particularly when that 'grinding and polishing' that is spoken of in St. Augustine's sermons, is taking place 'endlessly' in the world. I feel at peace with you, Lady, at one with you. Writer or no writer, winner or loser, I do feel at one with you, my friend and loved one, as I do with Haggard, Steersman and Tewfik Man."

She nods and says nothing. She touches me and I shiver. I shiver concretely and I know her power. She touches my forehead, she touches the place in my neck and in my lower back where the pain and illness are. I grow quiet, feeling her care and love. I soften, the tears are near but do not come.

"No matter," she says. I think that she is going to add, "We are together," and I cringe a little. I do not want this dialogue to be with "anima" or with the "feminine-in-search-of-relationship-nothing-else-matters." I want this to be body-psyche union, that is what I want, and that our relationship, hers and mine, be that union in healing, in writing and creativity!

She smiles, understandingly. All will be well. But, I think, so much illusion is still here. So much.

It is two or so days later, and I need to continue the hated "reportage," because of the simple need for continuity of "story" in this soap opera. Yesterday afternoon I spent with the lawyer, going over the new contract he drew up for the publisher. This would give me much more power and control. I would own the plates, the paper, the books and, if I need to pay for it, the binding of the first run. If the publisher goes bankrupt, furthermore, I am not responsible for it, since it becomes a personal agreement. It is as if I am the owner of the book and he is licensed to publish it. But the attorney was doubtful whether the publisher would sign it as it is. We have little or no leverage. In any case, it looked a bit gloomy and another instance of deception, futility, and my own stupidity, rendering me powerless.

That night — last night — I had an impressive dream, which I will go into later on, but I awakened in a sad, frustrated, failed state. Powerless, foolish. Then I went to the publisher's where I met the attorney as well. To our amazement, the publisher was not loathe to sign the new agreement. It was not only foolishness on his part, since he read it carefully. Perhaps he did not really understand it all, but he signed it just the same! That gave us some encouragement. D again said that a big check was clearing and would be available in a day or two, so he would now not only be able to pay for the binding, but to get some ads also. Well, I am hardly convinced of the latter, but I did strongly indicate that I wanted those books out soon and wanted to see and arrange with the bindery to deliver them as soon as possible. I had previously talked with the man, who told me he would not proceed until he received the money.

Well, D and I went down to the bindery and the man struck me as sound, a traditional sort of craftsman, with integrity. He agreed to proceed at once on the basis of my assurance that I would pay if D did not, and now, in two weeks time, the books will be there!

So then, the 80 people who have already bought the books will receive them, the 300 other orders will receive theirs, too, and I will have them for my friends and for the reviewers I know of. D spoke of other reviews he had arranged, but I take that, of course, *cum grano salis*. I felt for him, though, having to go through a three-day hospital stint, to fight off the doctor's recommendation of surgery and to keep going in his weakened condition until September, when his medical condition should change, astrologically. He is a good astrologer and he is trying to live his own life by it, so I can empathize with him there. But all my frustration with his delays and exaggerations plus lies had hardened me to him. Now, no longer feeling so totally powerless with him, having a good contract and a date by which the book must appear, I feel more benevolent. I have suffered humiliation and pain, but perhaps this, too, has been necessary.

It was with great pleasure that I phoned my parents just now and told them the good news. They, particularly, feel the need for my "role," but not in an unloving way. It was good for me, too, to talk with my father about his humiliations. But he was not bitter at all, being the joyful person he is. He repeated to me, however, just as he did a few weeks ago, that dark news came just after we had given him and my mother the big 50th anniversary present of a trip to Israel. He had said that when things are going very well, "look out!" a small bomb is likely. That from a man who has enjoyed life thoroughly, been full of humor, purpose and positive philosophy, has let much trouble "roll off his back."

My wife just called and I was happy to tell her the good news, particularly after this morning when I was both crying and laughing with her about a dream I had had. So my friends and loved ones share my good fortune, as they have shared the bad, and I am glad. This leads me to write about the dream I had last night — the potentiation of the impotent Magician!

In the beginning of the dream, I am in an office doing therapy. It is not my actual office, but is a room which neighbors on a larger living room and other rooms, much like our present use of the little house. I am working in the dream with two women simultaneously, but there are distractions. People come in and out. I take this as good-naturedly as I can, since I seem to have no other way of handling this. At one point my son is also there, and an attractive woman — not a patient of mine, I think, but looking something like one I worked with long ago — is flirting with him. She is rubbing his neck and talking huskily to him. I am thinking that it would be a nice thing for him if she did, indeed, take him under wing and teach him a bit since she seemed quite nice and loving.

As this is going on, there is a commotion in the other room and even more people come in. I am informed by a serious young man that a great Guru wants to see me, and this is quite an honor. He is ready to take me as a pupil, something he has refused to do with others for many years. I am startled by this, since I did not ask for a Guru but I am certainly willing to meet this person. Will he come here? No, he is too big and great to come here, I am to meet him nearby, outside. I go with the disciple to meet the great Guru, in a somewhat austere nature area. There, some fifty feet away, standing next to a large boulder, is the Guru. He looks Hindu, with a dark face, very intense eyes, and wears a loose, white robe, something like the clothes I remember seeing in India when I was there as a young sailor.

The Guru comes toward me with large strides, and I hold out my hand to greet him as he approaches me. He takes my hand as he comes up to me, but hardly do we touch when he explodes in great affect. The explosion is very high energy, and in the next moment I see him several yards away, but now in a different form. Now he is a small woman with very strange eyes and mien. At the same time, the arm is shaking my hand very vigorously. He is apparently quite angry with me, but is also demonstrating his *siddhis*, his powers. I am wondering what it is I did wrong. This has to do with my formality, in part, and I wonder, is it also that I am not respectful enough? In a way, I am a little amused by his intensity and slightly hysterical emotion, as has been uproariously caricatured by the great comic, Peter Sellers. But in the dream as in reality I know that this amusement is in no way disrespectful, since I am sometimes amused at my own intensity and slightly hysterical manner when I am involved as a teacher. Why could this Guru be so offended by that, or by formality? Shaking hands?

My reflections in the dream are interrupted by the power of the *siddhis*, and I am wondering what I am to do. I am aware that I had been occupied with the problem of illusion, both in life and in magic, yet I clearly feel the power of what he is doing, as I stand there, shaking a hand which is also shaking mine very slowly, while the rest of this person, in female form, is several yards away, looking at me strangely, moaning. I feel the powers, certainly, and wonder if I am expected to kneel.

Then the dream changes, and I am brought back to a more ordinary level of dreaming, walking down a city street. I walk down a street like Wilshire Boulevard in Los Angeles and see Seymour, a psychiatrist I knew when I began my internship many years ago. He is standing on the back of a fire truck and is wearing a uniform of a fire chief. Several other fire chiefs are with him, and he is apparently going to speak to them about psychiatry and fire-fighting. I am pleased to see him after all these years. He looks well. I go up to him and greet him, shake his hand. He shakes, but is pre-occupied with his role and the fire chiefs, so I move away a little.

Now I am talking with a man or several men about the problems of fire-fighting. One of these is a helicopter pilot. The men have decided whether, when they come from an underground storey to fight a fire, they should run the two hundred yards or be picked up by the helicopter. There seems to be an energy and financial question here. As I hear about this issue, I think it not so very important, but I wake up feeling downcast and defeated. My thoughts are about money, being cheated, stinginess, but then they go to the Guru and to the psychiatrist. I am so defeated by the powers, whether inward and magical (like the Guru), or outer and (like the psychiatrist) institutional. I offer my hand, am open and friendly, but apparently these are not the right thing.

So, I am sad and, as I do my morning exercises, thinking of the coming meeting with the publisher and this dream, I start to sob. When I think of the Guru as Peter Sellers, though, and am aware of the paradox of the seriousness and ridiculousness of the whole thing, I also laugh. My wife is there to share these feelings with me, and she embraces me warmly. I feel her lovingness as she offers me her views. I am too open perhaps, she says, or maybe the Guru is already teaching me, like a Zen Master, and it is no real defeat ... Perhaps. But there is the dream, and there too are the events of the morning. I feel as if another corner has been turned, and now I can/must continue on my way.

What is my understanding of this dream? The question, indeed, seems to be a paradox, the continuing problem of the "two's." There are two women patients, and now even my son (a younger, innocent, and well meaning version of me?) is getting into the work. There is the two-sidedness of the Guru-Magician, the two sidedness of my reaction. I recall the great Crown dream too. After I slew the fire-spitting dragon, I also walked an ordinary city street. This theme and even the fire continue: power and impotence, being singled out and rejected, greeted warmly and ignored, being great and nothing, famous and insignificant. The problem of the opposites and of the paradox goes right on, as it has all my conscious life, since my analysis began at age twenty-four and since the hero myth began at the age of three. It is a problem of fire and how to deal with it; the problem of passion, intensity, the heat and light of the sun which I felt at three, at twenty-four, at forty, and now at forty-eight; but it never let up!

I know the collective, institutional approach to fire as represented by psychiatrists. I am friendly toward it now, though I fought it at twenty-four and was rejected by it at forty. It tends to ignore me, of course. And the Guru-Magician part of it? It reminds me of the Magician dream I had some years ago. Then a great Persian Magician on a colorful magic carpet was next to me, several feet off the ground, while I, too, was on a magic carpet, but a smaller one in black and red (typewriter ribbon!). He approached to embrace me, with his huge power, but I was defensive. I understood that Magician, then and after, as a creative power which went into my writing the third volume of my trilogy, *The Love*. But the Magician power is still there to be reckoned with on another level, now as Guru.

I guess I do not approach that right either, even though I am friendly. This Magician, at any rate, is far from impotent, as I feel that I am, and can surely demonstrate his powers. Are these the powers I feel as a teacher?

An old friend and colleague, B, has come by, and we have talked about these matters. We have both struggled with similar issues of passion, of relationship, the spirit and flesh, but our intellects and feeling-functions are different. He noted that in my dream, therapy concerns are at the beginning and end and, importantly, that I meet the Guru outside, in nature and the world. Thanks for the observation.

Right now, I feel stopped. My friend describes his writing as labored, slow. My productivity is high, but is it creative? I said that I wanted to feel more of a sense of integration in the moment, pursuing the momentary state of what feels good and right (after duties and obligations are met), rather than the endless struggle for wholeness, such as is envisioned by Jung. That hero quest has always been for me like Jacob wrestling with the Angel, both doing God's Will and battling Him — all in the service of realizing the being of the Self on earth and in man. Now however, after all these failures I am equally interested in integration in the way that my wife enjoys, following the well-being of the moment. Perhaps greater attention to the lesser passions might lead to better "fire-fighting," better control of the intensity before it reaches flaming states of passions which destroy.

But now I feel no more like writing — to follow my stated intention of the last paragraph — and want to read in Magic (by Crowley), and perhaps do some physical stretches and a walk. Good! That is what I want (need?), so I do it!

Later, I address the Tewfik Lady:

"Madam, I have talked with my wife and am convinced that the Way of Well-Being in integration is something I need, in contrast to my traditional Way of Struggle. I have always been like Jacob with the Angel of God, struggling with that spirit so that he might bless me. In that, I have followed the heroic Knight's path of battle with the dragon and powers, but have 'armored' myself thereby. In my childhood, that knightly, solar place included a fear of the feminine. Now perhaps, I can embrace the feminine even more and find that Way of Well-Being, as I now call it. What do you think?"

"I think that you talk too much."

"Oh, no! Again, just like an *anima*! And I thought that you were more than that, a true being of the body-psyche, a spirit of flesh, as you averred."

"I am."

"Yes, I know. And talking, of course, can be an evasion of sensing, feeling, being."

"Yes."

"But, dear Lady, I accept that. You know all that I have said already. (She nods). I am more interested in making this knowledge and view manifest in my being."

"That is easy," says Tewfik Woman.

"Easy?" say I. "Easy, perhaps for you, but not for me."

"Easy for you, also," she answers. "You must only follow what you preach: listen from moment to moment."

"All right ... Let me listen, even now, as I talk to you and try to relate to you, to what is happening with my body and sensations, an awareness of cells ... I feel fairly comfortable, although there is some radiation of energy and a slight pain down my right arm. It increases. I also start to feel sick to my stomach and have a headache which comes and goes quickly ... Have you a comment?"

"No, I do not. I shall show you my own sensation." At this point Tewfik Woman begins to stroke her own skin, sensually. She rubs her arms and breasts, and brings her hand to her nose, and sniffs as if she has found a true ambrosia: a perfume of delight in her own body. I think that she is saying that she delights in her body, where I struggle and am sickened by my own. She nods in response to my stating this.

Now I sigh. It is true, and that is what I want to change ... I watch her further. Now she looks into my eyes deeply and smiles. Her lips are red and attractive, slightly open. My own breath, however, possibly smells bad as does my tasting. I feel a darkness in my body-spirit and she is with a light one. She smiles once more. She takes my head between her two hands, and looks into my eyes.

"Like a mother am I," she says, "to cradle your face and body in a loving way."

"Like a son am I," I respond, "accepting your love, and listening with rapt attention to your teaching. I abandon my strength, my knowledge, and defer to yours. But be not, pray, one more 'anima image' as of old, which in the working leads to change in the spirit, but not in the flesh! Teach me, dear Lady, to be a lover of the flesh-spirit in myself."

" 'Teach me,' says he," continues Tewfik Lady, speaking to I know not whom, perhaps my other friends. "He does not remember that he is here in Tewfik Land to teach as well as be taught, to be honored as well as to honor."

"I remember, Tewfik Woman. At this moment, though, I feel that I have nothing to teach."

"Your being here is information enough," she responds. "Have you already forgotten your experience with the unexpected change in Tewfik Green? And just by your presence? You have only to be here in order to help us and our way. Do you notice that, again, you need only 'be'?"

"I notice and remember."

"Come then and be. Bring your friends, Haggard and the Steersman. We shall leave for now my compatriot, Green Tewfik Man, and go once more to my land of Orange Tewfik to delight in a new aspect of it. This is not for him at this time since he might contaminate it by his green. I do not mean this reproachfully, but as a simple fact."

Tewfik Green Man nods in acquiescence to this statement of his compatriot in Tewfik Land. He bows, vanishing into a blank space. Now Haggard and Steersman and I are once more in

Tewfik Orange. We walk on that orange earth, and it is even more spongy than before — or perhaps we feel it more. We walk slowly and heavily for a bit and then lie down. Why are we here, I wonder, and what is it that she wishes to show us?

Now I see her jumping up and down on this spongy land in a most ungraceful, but humorous way. That is not what I expected from this beautiful, agile woman with the sensual and flowing movements. What is she trying to demonstrate? Up and down she goes with bent knees, like a clown. She does a dance of clumsiness, but with some pleasure. I do not know what she means by it. She finally stops and breathes heavily, her chest heaving. She seems to take pleasure in breathing itself. Does she mean to say to me, that is how I am: working like hell, trying to wear out my body, expend energy, and then enjoying the rest? She nods ... But I already knew that. Why show this again? Now she pouts a little, unhappy that I am not pleased by her methods, or what she is trying to teach ... Sorry, I think, but I already know this ... Then teach me, she seems to say, without further words from her.

"I cannot teach you, fair Lady," say I. "And I regret to say that you are now teaching me something I already know."

"Did I not say that before?" she answers.

So she did, I recall. She said — or implied — that I already knew the answers. All right, I shall give up the "being taught" syndrome, if I can. But what of my friends, Haggard and the Steersman? What do they wish in Tewfik Orange Land? I see them, but they have dimmed in my mind and vision.

I feel sick once more — as if this writing is not real. More illusion and more foolishness. I feel sick at my stomach. My arm aches and I want to cry, but I take a deep breath and feel better. I think of the woman's graceless dance and her deep breath, and I understand. Even my graceless writing and my jumping up and down in it, leads to a deep breath and to relaxation.

Tewfik Woman smiles broadly, hugs me. I have gained a bit.

Later, I "happen" to read a little essay by Crowley, the great Magician, on the Law of Liberty, which is: "Do What Thou Wilt! That is the Whole of the Law! Love is the Law, Love Under Will." Let me quote a bit of what he says:

Then comes the first call of the Great Goddess Nuit, Lady of the
Starry Heaven,
who is also Matter in its deepest metaphysical sense,
who is the infinite in whom we all live and move and have our
being.
Hear her first summons to us men and women:
'Come forth, O Children under the stars, and take your fill of love!
I am above you and in you. My ecstasy is in yours.
My joy is to see your joy.'

Later she explains the mystery of sorrow:

'For I am divided for love's sake, for the chance of union.'

And what are her conditions of love and peace and glory, to be
contrasted with the gloomy asceticism of the Christian, Buddhist,
and Hindu (to paraphrase Crowley in this)?

Be ye goodly therefore; dress ye all in fine apparel; eat rich foods
and drink sweet wines that foam!
Also, take your fill and will of love as ye will!
But always unto me.

Crowley points out that:

This is the only point to bear in mind, that every act must be a ritu-
al, an act of worship, a sacrament. Live as the kings and princes,
crowned and uncrowned, of this world have always lived, as
masters always live; but let it not be self-indulgence; make your
self-indulgence your religion.

"Those are his comments, Lady of Tewfik Land," I say. "I think
that his experience of the Great Goddess, Nuit, Lady of the
Starry Heaven who is also Matter in its deepest metaphysical
sense, is much like my experience of you, Lady of Tewfik Land.
She even describes herself as the 'blue-lidded daughter of
Sunset,' as well as the 'naked brilliance of the voluptuous night-
sky'! Is that you, Tewfik Lady, Orange Lady of Orange Tewfik
Land? Is that you?"
"It is not I," she replies. "But she is as my sister of another
realm, another realm where the Crowleys of this world and the

other worlds may meet her. I am what I have said, Marvin, a member of Orange Tewfik Land, not even its Queen. It is true, that her message is much like mine, but is different, too; as Crowley is different from you."

"He is indeed, I hope. In the photographs of him, he looks something of a lush: unpleasant, a bit fat and lascivious, more than usual. But perhaps I am prejudiced. He writes truly and well in this essay, and to the point."

"Accept it then, without cavil."

"I do. I quietly seek the state you describe ... Enough. I await a further dream."

A few days later. It is Monday, and I am down. At the moment, the book struggle seems to be resolved: in only some ten days it will be bound and I will see it as a living reality. But the acceptance of my spirit is still uncertain.

At the same time, I feel more love toward and from my wife than ever, if that is possible. We are so close, so warm. I am very lucky to have someone I love and who loves me, after more than twenty-one years of marriage. But I am depressed anyway. In one sense, I should be following the Way of Fulfillment and Gratification, the Way of Well-Being as I called it, as my wife does. Am I? In writing? I am writing in the old way, looking for help, understanding, teaching from the unconscious. Am I looking for something in the wrong place? Or, on the other hand, in struggling with depression, am I following the Way of Struggle? Am I writing because I want to, have the need, where it is part of the Way of Well-Being? That was the sense of Haggard and the Lady of Tewfik; that I would like to fulfill. I do not want to merely fall back into the old style of active imagination.

My writing has begun to hint at the Magician, with that Guru and fire-fighting dream, along with the Crowley reading. Instead of looking for help from the unconscious, from my friends in Tewfik Land and Haggard, perhaps I should enquire of them, see how they are doing? That would be an innovation, although, in the past, in active imagination *à la* Jung, I have done this, just to see the state of the unconscious, not in the service of the relationship itself. I think that a relationship asks for contact "for itself," as my colleague, B, says too. Enough. How are my friends in Tewfik Land?

I see them resting on the yellow-orange, foam rubber ground of Tewfik Orange. The Steersman, looking dark, like the Arab on that strange adventure, lies flat on the ground, resting. But no, he is not that Arab; rather he looks like the Guru of my dream. Or is it he? I look about some more. I have a sense of Haggard, dressed in his suit and handsome with his mustache, but he is more "present" in spirit than there on the ground of Orange Tewfik. And the Lady of Tewfik, and the Green Tewfik Man, are they there? ... Haggard speaks:

"I am here, Marvin, and pleased that you come and see us. As far as I know, the Tewfik People are gone for the moment and we are left, you and I, with this man who claims he is a Guru. I do not know if he is our Steersman or not, since I too have been sleeping. But he does look like that Arab chap who took on a life in our story, does he not? But I am a little confused in all this myself. Shall we wake him and see what it is he wants?"

"I am not sure it is wise to wake him, Rider, since he seems to be rather irritable and flighty. It is strange though, that he should be both a Guru and look like the Arab. As if Mercurius, that Angel, changes in so many ways as we approach him, that it is most difficult to relate to him. I have been depressed again, and I wonder if this 'down' from an 'up' is also connected with him."

As I talk to Rider, I see the eye of the Guru open, and he smiles. He looks more like Peter Sellers now. He sits up and starts speaking with an Indian-English accent — rather, his mouth is formed that way, although no words come out! Haggard and I both start laughing at this. Whatever it is, it is a good antidote for my depression ... Now the Guru, still looking a little like Sellers, smiles some more, throws a scarf about his neck, and pokes fun at the romantic, heroic image. Haggard and I look at each other and smile. We both have been guilty of that. But why is he poking fun at us and also trying to make us laugh?

"Because you cry so much," come whispered, lip-formed words without sound from this Guru.

"I don't cry a lot, Guru, but I do moan a great deal," say I, sighing shamefacedly.

"And I am not exactly guiltless of that boring self-concern, I must say," adds Haggard.

"Well then," says the laughing Guru, "well then." He resumes his prone position, closes his eyes, and is soon asleep. Now he looks like a true Hindu rather than an actor.

I wonder why he gave us that little message? But then I am back in that questioning, pining mood. I feel ridiculous in this writing now, where it should be merely more active imagination and not numbered pages, pretending to be a book. In other words, back in my complex of sadness, worry, self-criticism, lack of creativity. I look over at Haggard, who is still smiling. He, at least, has not fallen into the swamp ... Swamp. I remember it in that monastery dream, and I think that the swamp is sometimes fertile and full of rice, sometimes changes to a beautiful garden, and sometimes is just as I think it: smelly, sticky, dark and depressing. Self-indulgence. But that may be the necessary fertile ground of the artist, where he must dig anew ...

At that point, the Guru opens his eyes, looks at me and yawns. He is bored with me, just as I get bored with myself in this swamp state ... But now the Lady appears in a nice halo of orange and walks over to the Guru. She bends over his resting form and peers down at him into his sleeping eyes. He opens one and winks at her, at which point she starts to laugh. She comes over to me, takes my hand, saying:

"This Guru is nothing but Peter Sellers, the actor. He is no Guru!" Then she pauses for a moment and says, "But then, he may be, if he can teach you to laugh. Particularly at yourself!"

"Well," say I, "I do laugh at myself fairly often. If I laughed even more at myself, that would be the end of the Hero, the Crown, the writing, the whole thing, I guess."

"No, no!" Orange Tewfik Lady exclaims. "Not that! We mustn't give that up, lest we all fade away into a mere dream! That will never do."

I sigh, not knowing *the* answer, *an* answer, or anything else. Here I am, with a lovely lady who calls herself Spirit of Flesh, with the famous dead writer, H. Rider Haggard, with a Guru who may or may not be Peter Sellers, the actor — all this talent, genius, and beauty ...

"Well?" asks one of this number. "Well?" they all ask. Well what? I think. What are they asking? Are they asking me what I should do with it all? Are they asking why I get so down and skittery, perhaps like the hysterical Guru himself? "What are you asking of me, my friends?"

"You know the answer for me already," says Haggard. "Merely friendship, and a joint quest into the problem of art and the occult, that is enough for me."

"And for me, Marvin," says Lady of Orange Tewfik, "it is enough to honor you, have you honor me, and to fulfill the promise of the coronation."

"And you, Guru, or Peter Sellers, or Mercurius, or Steersman, whichever and how many of these you are, what do you want of me?"

The Guru yawns, and goes back to his feigned sleep. Now I do not know what to do. Partly, I am drawn back to duties or reading, but I feel a little better, it is true. I am less depressed than I was. I am grateful to the funny Guru-man. But, do my friends Haggard and Lady Tewfik have any requests? Haggard shakes his head. Lady Tewfik closes her eyes sensually. I go over and embrace her. I now feel even better. I wonder where the Green Tewfik Man is. I see him lying down on the Orange Tewfik turf of foam, amused at all of this. He has no needs either. So I return to reading Crowley.

... I finish reading Crowley on Magic and have mixed emotions about his Law of Thelema: Do What Thou Wilt. An exercise in redemption via White Magic, the seeking of self-knowledge and fulfillment in joy; the rejection of the Black Magic of Despair and Sorrow, not as a truth, but as something to be overcome. These I like, but his style, his arrogance and above all his looks, fill me with disgust. But, following what he says (Jung said it better), I shall follow my own Guru, my own path to fulfillment. Not much luck yet, I say to myself, but the final returns are not in yet!

In the reading, I slept once and felt quiet, as if the way of Tewfik Lady was being fulfilled also. But what of this Guru with his *siddhis* and emotion? Will he take my hand and not become hysterical? ... I offer it, and he smiles. My thoughts return to rejection, to anger at not being rewarded for being one's self. Well, I say to myself, it is all right. There is a risk of rejection by others, by their not wanting this person that you are. But that is all right ... The Guru nods, says nothing. But I am down.

Later. I think that I know why the Failed Artist, the Unpublished Writer, is hurting. I have called D, and there is still no repair of his telephone. I have called his neighbor, and no one have seen him. I have a contract now, the book will be finished, but I guess I hoped/believed that he did get his check, that his phone bill would be paid, and that he would be in a position to mail out my books when they are finished.

I have just called the hospital that he mentioned, and they say that he has not been there! My God, more illusion? Even in that? Well, stout heart. I will own the books at any rate. The people who have ordered them will get them, and I can at least peddle the rest myself! But still, sadness. Always defeat: body, soul, spirit! Illusion, in one way or another. Do I want to talk to my friends? To Haggard, the Steersman, Tewfik Lady or Tewfik Man? No. Disheartened. Read.

Days later. Still the sad writer. No word once again from D, although I left word with his neighbor; his secretary also. But why should I be surprised? He practically never leaves word for me, never returns calls, never keeps me informed. Each time I encounter his lying, irresponsibility, or deceit, I feel wounded. But each time there is some forward movement on my book, I resume my hopes, expectations, understanding, compassion for him. I suppose that I must maintain this illusion or just be too defeated and self-recriminating. Should his hospital stay be also a lie and should his receipt of the money be one as well, I shall have to simply make use of the new contract and take over the book. But if those are lies, then it is also a lie that a book club was interested. I will be left with a thousand books, some eighty already paid for, several hundred on order, with perhaps seven hundred not accounted for. That, plus no way of distribution that I know of, the additional expenses of binding, of the dust jacket, of mailing. All that, plus the continuing shock of illusion. Too much.

"Oh my friends, Haggard and Steersman, Lady and Man of Tewfik Land, where are you now? You were certain that all would be well. I wonder if you still are. Even as I write, I have more illusion, more fantasy. I think that this, too, is part of the process, that further defeat will be repaired by success; that my books will appear, and that even this crying, distressed account of a failed writer will appear and somehow give courage to some other frustrated, failed writer, make him and her feel hope and not give up. That comes to me as a meaning for this despair, frustration, and illusion. The meaning is one of persistence and sharing the agony, for it is a common one. How many writers are defeated! How many artists are failed in one way or another? Most, I suppose. Even the successful ones.

But what of the artist's narcissism, his worries, self-concerns, self-involvement, inflation, belief in his divine calling — all those things which I also feel. And why should anyone want to read about that? Unless he is an artist, a writer, and is reading those things in a book which is successful, and gives him hope!

So I continue. I could ask my friends in Tewfik Land to help find something which would make me feel more like a writer: a story. Rather, I need their help with the problem of success and failure, illusion. Are you there, my friends?

I see, instead, a sneering man whom I knew casually. A writer himself, he was also a psychologist and one who was given erroneous information by another psychologist that I, in my role as Director of Studies of the Jung Society, kept that man out. I did not do this, it was a decision of a larger board which I merely communicated; I was the bearer of bad tidings and thus the bad person. This other, a writer who has had a small measure of success (I think that two of his books were published) is sneering at me. He has his revenge. He puts me down. It is no matter that I was not guilty of the charge brought by his friend. It is no matter that my success or failure has little to do with this man, he sneers. Or so, of course, do I imagine him. The actual man probably has no idea of my present pain. He was present last year at Notre Dame when I spoke about my book, but it was due to come out last fall, as far as he knew, and I am sure he knows nothing of my present fate — at least at any rational level. It is possible that at an occult level he knows. And perhaps, Haggard, it is just such a place that interested you. I see Haggard now, dressed in his suit and impeccably groomed.

Haggard nods and is interested in this appearance of the sneering writer-psychologist. Is this a true occult phenomenon or a manifestation of my own sneering at myself? "Well, Haggard, let us see what this sneering writer-psychologist has to say. Perhaps we can see if it is my own self-hatred or whether it is related to the occult realm.

"What do you say, X?" say I. "Why are you sneering?"

As I say this, his face changes to sadness. "I am not X, as you thought," he says, "but your own hate and sadness. I am incarnated as a demon, a separate force which feeds itself on you. You created me and wished for me."

"Wished for you?" say I. "How did I do that?"

"You presented yourself, just as that psychologist did, and in your naïveté, like his, made yourself open to demons. So here I am, your created demon, arising out of the right conditions. I am sad, defeated, sneering, by turns. I am created out of your unhappiness and despair. Did you not once write that God created deserts with His own dryness and depression? Can you not create a little figure like me out of your own melancholy?"

"I suppose so. But why do you take the form of X?"

"Only to get your attention. And only so that you would raise the question of occult connections. It is occult enough, I dare say, that I can maintain a totally separate identity, without my having to be another existing person!"

"Yes, I can see that, although it raises some questions about the psyche, of course. One of these, really, is: have I done the same thing with my friend Haggard? Is he merely my own creation and has nothing to do with the true Haggard who lived, and breathed, and wrote?"

"That is not my concern, but yours and his. My concern is with you, my creator!"

"What is your concern, my creation? What do you want, you born out of my own despair, self-hatred, and illusion?"

Now I see Haggard draw closer, most interested. I glance at him to see if he responds to the idea that he is merely a creation of mine, that he is not Haggard himself. He seems to disregard this and is convinced that he has a separate reality, not my creation, just as he claimed earlier. But then, he too as my creation could be deluded! Since I am so easily deluded and confused, surely that which I might create might also think of itself as self-created, or having an independent existence, which it does not! But Haggard, seeming to know my thoughts as I think them, merely looks at me and smiles. He looks back to this angry writer and waits to hear what this fellow has to say. The fellow now becomes more ghost-like, less in the form of a person, and speaks:

"I am indeed a spirit. A spirit of writing. I am a creation of yours in so far as your writing spirit is defeated, self-hating, rejected and, in turn, performing these acts upon you. But I am, after all, a spirit, too, and not only created by you. My form and shape depends upon you, but my existence, my reality, does not. Let me explain. There is that in me which is independent of men, writers or not. It is the spirit that I am which appears to those who think they are writers or are informed of this fact by the gods. But the particular clothes that I wear, the molding of feeling, attitude, content and concern, are created by those very writers who summon me or are summoned by me."

Hearing this, I think of the genie in the bottle, of Mercurius, and I look to him again, the Steersman. He smiles, and I think, Oh God, another form of the changing Mercurius! That too is defeating, and does not bring me new information, a new way, new anything. It merely brings me back into my despair, uncertainty, and confusion!

Mercurius does nothing, but grows more serious. Now Haggard has less reality, as does the writer-spirit. And I am feeling more deeply my sadness, my feeling of nothingness in this work, my sense of defeat and foolishness. It is the Fool that I feel, another archetype, just like that of Mercurius and that of the Writer, as he describes it. Now I am identified with the Fool; not the creative, joyful, Aleph-energized figure of the Tarot cards, but the human, stupid fool who is so easily deceived, dismayed, brought to nought.

"Why do you want to do this to me, Mercurius?" I cry out. "Why do you want only to fool and deceive and play with us poor would-be writers? Why?"

No answer. All seems to fade. I am tempted to turn away from these inner pursuits and concerns and seek nourishment and understanding from outside my own fantasy, which merely beguiles and deceives me. Just like the outer world! ... That thought comes to me. Before it was just the outer world that was doing this to me; now it is the inner as well! Well then, where is my lawyer here? Where is my advocate before the most high

Mercurius who deceives me? Where is the new contract which would make him perform properly or leave me alone?

I call out these things, but there is no answer. I am alone. There is no help right now.

A few days later, I sit at my desk in a state of near madness. My head aches, partly I imagine, from the fasting I have been doing for almost 45 hours, partly from the crazy-making conditions I have been subject to. Yesterday it became clear that the publisher was a pure liar from beginning to end. He had not been in the hospital that he said he was going to, his phone was still out of order, and when I spoke to the printer, he informed me that the publisher was going into the hospital this weekend, that no money had appeared, that, in fact, he had never paid the printer for the time on the presses. It looked like all was over. I talked with the lawyer, and the only issue now was how to extricate myself as best I could.

Last night I was quite inarticulate with it all. I was so despairing about everything, the whole year had been sheer illusion. My wife was loving and sympathetic, but she used the word "humiliation." I did not think that was the chief feeling for me, although it was there also, but I realized that this was the most painful part for her. For me, rather, it centered upon illusion and deception from Self and others. What was the meaning of all this senseless lying, this horror? The night was horrible. During the day, however, I managed to recover somewhat by finding hope again. The hope revolved around finding another way to distribute the books, of recouping somehow, still hoping to find someone in the publishing profession who would validate me.

Well, with that recovery, I just received a call from D. Weird. He said that the money arrived, that he had talked with the bindery, that the books would be ready May 1, that he would pay for it, that the packages were ready to send the books out, that the printer was engaged to do the dust-jackets. And what about his hospital? He had been at the Veterans Administration, not the one he mentioned. What about his phone: was it fixed? No, he hated to do it, but he guessed he would. And the money? Yes, it had arrived. All earmarked for everything, but it had arrived. I should bring down the addresses that I had for the review copies, and so on. As if it will be all right, all will be well. Let me check with the bindery ...

The owner was not at the bindery, but a very nice Puerto Rican man spoke to me. Call tomorrow or Thursday, he said. Just after my wife called, concerned. I told her the news and she was happy with it. Her stomach had been churning all morning, and she had come to a similar place, namely that with all the struggle, there had been progress, that the book was close to appearing. Now, it is clearly May 1 as a deadline. Either the publisher produces, or I take over and find a distributor. A deadline closer to my birthday. Oh Lord, let my 50th year, my approach to the half-century, be more fulfilling, more joyful and less fraught with pain, with disillusion and despair, than I have had since I celebrated my 40th birthday and my writing began.

Two days more, and I have gone on a further trip. I have been very high — rising from that low — and feeling well and confident that May 1 would bring a final coming to birth of my "child," my much abused and rejected first child in art, *The Tree.* Today I called the bindery, to check up on what D, the Neptunian vague one (as some say, rather than the deceptive Mercurius that I see) said, and what do I hear?

Well, he said the book should have been ready Wednesday as we had originally anticipated, even a day earlier, but do you know what happened? No, I could hardly guess. Well, a week ago, a machine broke down, a most rare occurrence, and we had to call up a place in Chicago and ask them to make this part, which is a combination of old and new, manual and automatic, and send it to us by airmail. Normally this takes two weeks to make, they said, but they would hurry and send it now. And what kind of machine is this, I asked. Well, he said, it is a "rounder and backer" for the binding. Oh. And how long would it take when he received the rounder and backer? Well, a little while, a few hours to install it, and then just a couple of days to finish. If the part came in today, Thursday, or tomorrow, well then, we would meet the May 1 deadline. All right, I said.

And all right, I felt, yet stuck once again. Is there a new demon? If so, what demon is this? And why is he so intent upon delaying, preventing my book from appearing? First it was all those publishers rejecting it, forty of them. Then it was the type-setter, going mad in the middle of her work. Then it was D, the publisher, with his vagueness, deception, and — on his side — the failure of his money to come in. And now, with all the help and confrontation, there comes a new barrier. This one hits the machine itself! And what does it hit? It hits the "rounder and backer." The machine that will make my artistic child (its cover-ing, defense, presentation body), both round (whole) and strong (backer).

It seems weird to me, indeed. Until this moment, I have not truly considered that a demon was at work. I have approached the frustration as part of my growth process. Even during the last totally depressing incident, when I thought that the whole year and publishing venture was delusion from beginning to end, I came out of it feeling that the point of this collapse was a lesson to the remaining vanity that I had. It was as if — as St. Augustine had preached — my diamond self was being roughly polished and all the excess dead carbon, like the dregs of the oil press in his sermon analogy, was running down into the sewer. The narcissistic and vain one in me was being fired and cleansed.

But now I feel that it has not been only that process, true as it is, nor even that D has been the Mercurius, since he has been as much a victim as I. Suddenly I see the possibility of some partic-ular demon which is inhibiting this book from coming out. I see that I am in danger here of overemphasizing my book's collec-tive importance, that I am tending to personify and objectify a "force" where there are many smaller and more rational reasons for all this delay and obstruction, for example: the times not appropriate for my book until now, the typesetter having her own sickness, D's own ineptitude and victimization and, finally, the book itself not being that good or important. I understand these more parsimonious reasons, but I am not fully satisfied with Occam's razor here, accepting more plausible explanations and the least complicated. It is just possible that there is a demon afoot. If nothing else, I might see this demon from a Jungian standpoint as an archetypal factor which is working in the uncon-scious and therefore is not limited to the "within," but can mani-fest outside as well. Or indeed, it might be a demon proper as in Magic.

I was very high today, having come through all the agony of the Writer and found out about the "burning out" of my narcissism and vanity. I had also given a talk at the university, to the counseling center, replete with its Freudians and Existentialists, psychiatrists, psychologists, and social workers. I performed well but could not handle, to my own satisfaction, the problem of the disengaging Freudian, the old "objectivist," who refuses to engage. I am much better at it, but I can see — from my talks with L, too — that I am not able to disengage satisfactorily myself.

Regardie and I talked for half an hour — about my "high," about the publisher, about my spirit, and the world. He felt that D was more Neptunian than Mercurial. He was, indeed, vague and hard to pin down, but fundamentally honest and would perform. He did have the connections that he had said he did, according to Regardie's lady and, besides, if I were a bit more patient, my own Guardian Angel would bring to pass what I needed, that the book would come out in due course. I did not have that full trust, I told him, particularly after the disillusionments of the past nine years (since that horrific one with my Jungian colleagues), and particularly this past eight months with D. Does one need nine months of labor pains to bring an already born child into the world?

It is a Monday, and I sit, as I have on so many Mondays, in gloom. I am not as down as I was earlier in the day, but occupied with the "Book"; the delay, once again, in its appearance. I have spoken to the bindery man today, and he says that he spoke with the Chicago machine people on Friday, and that they would have the part manufactured by today or tomorrow. They need a day to install the part after it is received and will then resume. Hence, the vaunted May 1 deadline will not be met: it will be another week, at least.

What is all this? I have just completed the book by Roberts: *Seth, Nature of Personal Reality,* which says that demons exist only if you believe in them. Indeed, he says, belief is everything: one creates one's own reality is the theme. I shall consider this further when I take that seminar on Astral Travel; but right now, I want to plumb more deeply this question of the demon and the obstruction with my book. Is it an underlying belief of mine which is inhibiting it? My unworthiness, perhaps? I can not believe it. Perhaps though, as friends and loved ones say, I have too much of myself invested in the publication of the book, too much of a belief that this will change my place in the world, give me the recognition and vindication that I need. They think that I am wrong. Yet beliefs, says Seth, are what creates reality. If I believe this, perhaps it will occur. Confusing, once more.

I wonder where my inner friends are now: Haggard, Steersman, and the Tewfik people? And I wonder what they think about this newest interruption in the appearance of the book, particularly the Tewfik people who honored me, as if I had won a Nobel Prize! Are they there? Yes, if I want it!

Haggard is there, looking at me, shaking his head.

"Marvin, I marvel at your determination and courage. It is most outstanding. I think that I would have gone under with such disappointments and defeats long ago."

"Yes, I seem to keep on going, Rider; how, I do not know. Some other hope or expectation or understanding comes up to enable me to go on a little more. But now I am with the question of a demon in this obstruction. Do you think that there is a force or power or something else which opposes this appearance of my book? You, with your interest in the occult, may incline along that line. May I add, Rider, that I feel somewhat disappointed with you, too, since *Wisdom's Daughter* has not appeared as you promised, nor have you, lately, brought any new flare or story to our enterprise."

"What you say is true, Marvin, I regret to say, both about the occult and my failure to be more active in our work. I cannot report much about it right now, except to say that my work has been elsewhere, primarily. Although I am available to you, I do have many other projects as well, as you might imagine. But I would like to make up for my lack of involvement with you and our project. As to the demon theory, I have little to add. The only demons that I know of are not mere 'creations,' as your magician friend seems to think, but they have their own existence, just as he and you and I have ours. Why this particular obstruction is so

persistent, I cannot tell. Perhaps the Steersman knows the answer
to this."

We turn, Haggard and I, to the Steersman, to see if he can
provide further information about this obstruction to my book's
appearing. He shakes his head, not knowing either. Well then, I
think, what about the Tewfik people, the Green Man and the
Orange Lady? Do they have an answer? I turn to Green Tewfik
Man and he smiles very broadly.

"I know nothing of demons," he says happily.

"But why such a broad smile?" I ask.

"Only because you address me. I thought that you lost interest
in me, just as Haggard had lost interest in you."

"No, Tewfik Man, I had not lost interest. I had lost hope. I
seem to have hope only in the Orange Tewfik Lady, since she, at
least, had some link with matter directly and with the flesh particularly. I had begun to give up on all of you as further figments,
illusions, delusions of mine. I am near to tears once more. Can
you all imagine the pain and disappointment of these last years?
Nine years since I began writing, which came out of disappointment as well! And now there are further disappointments and
pains. It seems like most of my recent life has been like that.
Yes, I know that most people undergo these things, that life for
many seems to be endless trouble, interspersed with occasional
pleasure or fulfillment. That is so, even for my father who has a
great joy in life. I seem to know that, despite what teachers, such
as Seth, have to say. Still ..."

"Yes, I realize that," says the Green Tewfik Man. "But you
must remember, Marvin, that we have honored you, and that is
not a routine, ordinary thing."

"I try to remember, Green Tewfik Man, as I try to remember
the glories of childhood and youth, such as the crowning, gold
lions on chests of mail, and 'green' such as yours. I try to
remember, but that, too, vanishes at times. All illusion, it feels
like. But now I am concerned with the obstruction and the possibility of a demon-force against my book, for some reason. You
have no knowledge of this?"

"No."

"Do you, Orange Tewfik Lady? You with whom I had hoped
to come to a greater understanding of the spirit-in-flesh; do you
know of such a demon or force in this obstruction?"

"I do not."

"Then I am left here without any answer. None. I only endure, drag myself along. I can enjoy the small pleasures, endure the pains and disappointments, but nothing comes. O.K."

Another day. A little calmer now. But I have felt impotent and incapacitated, unable to write, to deal with the "demon" if he exists, or to bestir new hope.

My friend L is disbelieving of the bindery man. She thinks that it may well be part of a plot to get the bindery man to tell me these things, so that the publisher will have more time to raise money. She is angry with me and afraid for me to be so stuck, so paralyzed. I should go down and find out if the machine is broken; I should get busy and write letters to find out about distributors, since I will soon have the book myself, without the publisher. I should act, in short, to help my pain and paralysis. This is what she does, she admits, for her pain. I appreciate her care and advice, but I also feel yelled at. If you want to help me that way, do it yourself, I say. But she says my wife ought to. But my wife would not agree, I think; true, I later find out. Then I myself will go down and check! Fine.

And my pupil, a young black psychologist, says that I am too involved in achievement. I have done what I could, then let it be. If it is meant to happen, it will happen. Yes, they are both right: one suggests action, the other surrender. Both are right! And that is why I am paralyzed! How can one act and surrender simultaneously?

Last night I had a painful dream. I was with my wife at a mechanic's shop. I was trying to get my old Volkswagen fixed or started, the one that I had for eleven years, from my time in Zürich in 1956 until 1967 when I bought my present car. There was great difficulty in getting it fixed or started. A mechanic showed me a panel with four parts to it, each of which needed adjustment. I adjusted them, but even then it was hard to start the car, since we had no key. Frustration. End of dream.

Awake, I think of this ordinary, banal, painful dream. I can't get going, am stuck. But I am trying to start the "vehicle" of an old place, from the time when I was in Zürich, right up until the time I resigned from the Jungian Society. That old machine is hard to get going. Does this represent my old Jungian attitude, active imagination and working on the inner life? Yes, I think so. But that is the way I worked on myself for so many years. I believed that addressing the gods within would be effective in the outer world as well. So then, why do I try and resurrect this vehicle? I have, indeed, had my new vehicle, my sports car convertible, Karmann Ghia, which I still drive since 1967 and that, too, is no longer young, almost eight years! Just as my stories are that old also. My writing is connected with the current car, and that is bogged down. Do I buy a new car or refurbish the old? In my dream I am indeed far back. Why do I do this? Because I am lonely, defeated, missing the connection with a meaningful community? Yes. But I cannot be the prodigal son, either. That would be compounding my defeats. What then, inner friends? Steersman, Angel, you who have guided me in so many forms, I ask you to speak to me.

He is there, dark and smiling, wearing a sporty hat, something like that of the gondola boatmen in Venice, a colorful African shirt, and pants cut at the knee. In all quite American, Italian, and African. He smiles. but does not answer, except that his being is an answer. He guides and steers and joyfully goes his/our way. He is my Angel after all, is he not? He is jaunty, has something of the Italian (feeling and love and flare), of the African (laughter and body connection, nature and vitality), and of the American (dedication, hard work, practicality, freedom, individuality). All these has he. And all these have I — at times. Have I them now? I do, at this moment. I know better who and what I am and feel better about myself. I can hope and act, believe and surrender. It is non-verbal, like the Steersman, Guide of Haggard and me. He serves the One Beyond, is the One Beyond in me, and guides. I am at peace at this moment.

A little later. I have a touch of bad conscience about my dream interpretation. How can I just give up the past of Jung, Zürich, etc.? I am a committed Jungian Analyst after all, despite my innovations (which seem not too successful in the world, either), and my *excursus* into Reich and the body. Even the latter, for me, seems a logical and empirical extension of Jung into the areas not healed, i.e., the body. I have just been reading Marie-

Louise von Franz's book, *Number and Time*. That stalwart and brilliant follower of Jung, who has always dazzled me, brings up in my fantasy a question about my abandoning that old car, especially since a mandala of four-fold wholeness seems to be at the base of the operations. An adjustment of all four "parts" is needed, which I seem to be able to do. Four functions, I imagine. To adjust my functions is possible and even done. But I lack the "key" to get it started once more. Was that "key," that engenderer of energy and vitality and life, a union of feeling and meaning (intuition)? Is that lost, now that I have failed to achieve the "recognized" individuation and success that I anticipated? That, plus alienation from the Jungians, largely? I imagine so. Yet in my heart and in my books, of course, there is not only great acceptance and use of Jung's ideas, but his clear participation as a kind of chief Guru. So then what? Perhaps I can ask the inner von Franz what she thinks? Magic? No, this as an inner image, not the actual woman. Miss V.? I call out. She seems aggrieved.

"I grieve that you are no longer with us. You of such talent and promise. I grieve that you are not among the followers of Jung."

"I feel that I am, Miss V. Particularly in my writing, but also in my therapy I follow him very deeply. I merely add new areas, describe in other modes. Whether I really have new ideas or not is quite debatable."

"I am glad you think so. No one can transcend Jung."

"What? You think that? That seems ridiculous to me!"

"And to me. It is a failure of my own development. I seem to have been stuck with a master; you have gone beyond."

"But a moment ago, you criticized me for not being a part of the group; for 'going beyond.' "

"So I did, so I did. Is that not a part of my own ambivalence? As a follower of a master, I wish all to remain with him, particularly gifted ones, but I also recognize that I am caught in being a follower."

"And what of me in that? I recognize myself fully as a follower. I have no difficulty there. I can also see where Jungian psychology did not do everything for me, so I merely applied it afresh in my therapy, as Jung would suggest. I also have gone onwards. I feel no difficulty with that, either. The only difficulty

I feel is lack of recognition, group camaraderie, connection with a meaningful collective."

"In that, you are like Jung. He made his own group, of course, but was lonely until the end. Did you not know that?"

"No, I did not. He had so many people around him, so much adulation and recognition."

"But never enough. We women had to nourish him a lot."

"I suspect that my women friends and loved ones have had to do the same with me. Even me, who is far from being in the same class as Jung."

"That self-disparagement, even as comparison, is no use."

"I agree ... But where, then, knowing what you know, do you think that I have failed Jung or Jungian psychology?"

"As I have said. In not remaining with the collective."

"But they violated me. And besides, I am still a member of the International Association, as you know."

"Yes, I know ... Can you not accept your own loneliness?"

"No. I am clearly not as big a man as Jung. My inner vision, supporting me during the writing of my books, seems far more mundane, human, vulnerable, failing, now."

"So much the better. More human, more life, more toward the *unus mundus* that you long for so much."

"Do you think I am getting there?"

"I do."

"It is strange. I keep experiencing support now in these inner chats and much opposition from without. At the same time, the inner support makes my inner life less visionary, creative, unique! What a continuing paradox!"

"So it is for me, too. My work merely explicates Jung. Not as original as yours."

"What? I don't think so. Your work on Fairy Tales, on Apuleius, on Creation Myths, and now on Number, are wonderful! Mine are just small thoughts coming out of the transference work or on religion. Even my larger books of fiction are just human stories of individuation."

"Beautifully told."

"Beautifully told? I can accept that. Thank you. I should validate and value my own work, even where others can not. Jung must have done that. I remember when I was rejected by the Jungian 'Fathers,' that Jung and my grandfather came to me, in fantasy and rejoiced with me, accepted me, danced with me. I hope that, too, was not illusion."

"It is not illusion. (She seems teary). Jung has told me of you. He, too, is with you. Have faith, hope. Grieve not."

"Thank you. I will trust. And I will value what I have done. I will value even what I am doing now, be it writing or not. In that, I see I will redeem what was beautiful in the old car which I drove in that dream, and yet not be condemned to never leave it."

Another day and another depressing dream. In this one, I am stimulated, but the sequence of events has to do with daily life, ordinariness. It is not the daily round and certainly not the magic of the special moments of life during the day, but something else. I feel as if the psyche is once again bringing me down into ordinariness, banality, and it makes me sad. I had gone to bed asking for a deep, healing dream, but what I received was far different. Why am I now getting these messages from the unconscious that bring me into ordinariness? Yesterday I remarked, in speaking with my inner friends, that I felt a lot of support from the inner world, that the obstructions were outside. Today, after the dream, I am wondering what kind of support I am getting. I wonder, too, why the messages seem to be relatively shallow. I also think of the daydream of yesterday, when I found myself out in the harbor beyond the ships, somewhere above the waves, watching a small steamship like a *vaporetto* of Venice come by. It was very clear and real. I think I was in the Astral, perhaps. And then I saw a football coming toward me very rapidly, as if it were a punt or kick-off. I was reminded of an early dream in analysis as a young man. In it, there were games going on, volleyball, basketball and such, with men and women. Then I was in a football game and the ball was passed to me. I ran well but was tackled just before the goal. It was a feeling of defeat. Now I experience that a lot, the feeling of defeat just before the goal. I feel the ball again coming to me and I wonder.

In the beginning of Jungian analysis, I had to experience the defeat of the hero-ego when carrying the Self. Later, in the crowning dream, I rejected my carrying the Self as if I was a hero. In these last years, when I want the crown, the goal, want and accept the rewards of work, believing I have creatively served the Self, now it is denied! What a paradox! My dreams seem to bring me into ordinariness once more.

"Lady of Tewfik Land! You it is I wish to speak to. You, I feel, can share these feelings and concerns. The sense of impotence and sleepiness has diminished. I would continue on that project that you and I started a while ago, of uniting spirit and flesh in myself, with your help. Are you there?"

"I am here, in the speaking of the birds, in your memory of the old cabin in the woods where the hermit lived, in every vivid sensation of beauty, of intensity, of love."

"You are there? Are you then a Goddess after all or an *anima*, as Jung has described?"

"I am neither Goddess nor concept. I am the Lady of Tewfik Land, as you call me, but by no means the ruler of this land either. As I have said, you may, one day, meet our ruler. But you seem loathe to continue with me just now."

"I am, it is true. I float in and out of consciousness. I talk to you, turn to reading, fall into unconsciousness, wake with a start, return to you. I don't know where I am."

"Then rest and return when it feels right."

A couple of hours later. I have been bicycling with B, and we have talked of his struggle to find totality in his marriage and of my sense of pain in not being able to fulfill my creative spirit in the work-world. I had realized it to some extent, but have not found my fulfillment in professional life, in groups or society, commensurate with the power of the archetype which has given its energy to me. That seems a clear and an accurate statement, neither immodest nor modest, but true. B thinks that this is because of my view about sexuality. I have believed that God is also there — indeed that energy is, in part, derived from sexuality — a dangerous view, apparently.

"What do you think, Lady of Tewfik Land? You are a woman. You are not a Goddess, you say, but you are not of this

earth, since you style yourself a 'spirit of flesh.' What do you say
to these reflections and doubts?"

"I do not know the details of that of which you speak, nor do I
know the theories of you or your friends. I know only that sex is,
indeed, a God, if you like, a power, and it must be viewed that
way or lost. You have viewed it so, hence the God has remained
with you. You have fought it, I know, and attempted to transform
it, humanize it, keep it in human and acceptable paths, but this is
only partly possible. The God, as you know, always has his own
aims. Better then to treat it as a God and both go with it and
restrain yourself, as you have tried to do. The God can ask no
more of you than that: you submit and worship and also hold
your humanity and its values."

"I agree with you. Or, maybe, my views echo yours and vice-
versa. But there are other issues in this. For example: the God we
are talking of now, I think, is the power of Phallos, that Dionys-
ian passionate one. We are also implying Eros, that equally
passionate one who also seeks union and flow, in addition to the
power and penetration and adoration of Phallos. Then there is
Aphrodite, of course, and … But I do not wish to enumerate the
Gods and powers. I wish to point out, though, that the Gods
themselves, associated with sex and love, may be in conflict, as
we well know. Phallos, say, in struggle with the Judge (Hera) or
the passionate joys of Aphrodite versus the family coziness of
Hestia, to name two. Besides that, I have raised the question of
acceptance in the world as well. And you have said nothing
about that."

"But Marvin, that acceptance question seems to be with you
all the time, in every way!"

"Yes, but B is suggesting that the one is because of the other!
That the reason for my non-acceptance is because of where I am
with the sexual issue. I do not accept myself, so I cannot be
accepted in the world, is his view. My friends might accept me,
but not the collective in this. So he says."

"Well, maybe he has a point, all right. That seems to be the
case. But I imagine that most women would not disagree with
you privately, however strong they publicly speak for the Hera
position, as you call it."

"Some do, of course, but few, to my knowledge. Most do not.
Or even if they agree, it is only as long as something untoward

does not happen to them, with 'their' man! Right? It seems to be a question of property or possession, not love."

"Right. But if you know so much about these things, then why approach me as an authority?"

"Because you are female, you are a 'spirit of the flesh' and this is a very high place, indeed. This union of spirit and flesh is much more important to me than sexuality alone, since there are also other aspects of impulse (food and drink and aggression, for example), as well as all those occult, subtle body places, that require an answer and a fulfillment. I would think that one who is 'spirit of flesh' would be of great help in these areas."

"Now you flatter me. Neither flattery nor devotion will achieve these answers for you — from me."

"What then, Lady of Tewfik?"

"You have the answers, my friend. We already agree. I do not think that the acceptance will come, at least on the terms you describe it. This will be gradual and, I imagine, based primarily on your own self-acceptance, independent of what the world thinks. If you and your Self, if Phallos and Judge can agree, then it will not matter so much what the world thinks. I know that it is important to you. It is not enough that we of Tewfik Land honor you but it will come to pass. We know that, too. But how and when, that is a time problem, one that we cannot answer."

"You support and reassure. I imagine, though, that if someone were to read this, they would say, 'they sure support him all the time, but what new is being said?' "

"Not much, I suppose," says Orange Tewfik Lady, laughing, "but what would you have us say? There is nothing new that we have to offer just now. You have the answers to these questions, and where you do not, neither do we!"

"All right. I suppose it is 'just so' that I work more towards self-acceptance, a union in myself, and let the rest find its own way. I have discovered that when I enquire about where people are, whether they agree or are offended or judging, then I feel all right with myself. It is only their terrible withdrawal that is so painful. And yet, I do not know how and when to withdraw myself! But enough. I shall not burden you further with my complaints and questions."

"It's no burden, Marvin, it is, as you say, 'just so.' "

"All right, then."

This is the next day. At the moment, I am feeling rather well, although I woke up in another state of gloom. The reason for the latter is because of the depressing dream I had. I gave myself the suggestion that I would have a deep, helpful dream, healing in nature, but I dreamt as follows:

A woman architect is struggling with an older man, her father possibly, who is also an architect. There is great competition between them. He is holding out for his designs and she has her own in mind. The old man is certainly not very attractive but she, too, seems not all that wonderful. She is rather sneaky. As I glimpse the structure of what she has in mind, I see a large, many-storied building which is quite open all around. It seems unfinished, only structural. I wake up from the dream feeling neither revived, healed, nor with greater understanding or depth.

I told this dream, and the one about the Volkswagen of a few days ago, to L this morning and, as I told it to her, I began to get a glimmer of what was happening. I got a greater perspective by telling it. It is as if my psyche is not healing me or giving me nice messages, but is rather telling me what is going on; namely, that the old psychology and structure (the old man), is not giving up so easily and that the new (the daughter), is trying, but also has questionable sides to it. L added some very valuable things, however. For one thing, she pointed out that the old condition is also the old morality, with its views of sexuality, ethics, and so on, which probably just will have to die, but is wreaking real havoc on its way out. She mentioned some examples from her situation also. Further, the noted Architect, seen from a Kabbalistic view, is the one who establishes "forms," structures which will be manifested at a later date. It seems that there is a struggle with these forms and the psyche is registering it. If I could just surrender, let the battle go on, no longer fight and struggle, it might be easier for me. L, for example, follows the "Way of Pleasure and Integration" through doing what feels right at the moment and does not fight it. I find it difficult to do that, but it would be a good thing, of course. I felt relieved and helped by her consciousness, by what she said, how she said it, and the fact that her awareness connects to where I am in spirit better than anyone else. It is very soothing for me. I breathe better after I speak with her.

Later, I spoke to the bindery man, who told me that the part was sent out by the factory in Cincinnati and it was quite a strange happening. This was the first time in 30 years that the machine, or any machine of his, had broken down, even the first time he had heard of such a thing. Further, he added, he found another breakdown in the machine, the tooth of a gear! This tooth was being repaired locally and should be all right today. He is a decent man, I think, not in cahoots with D to deceive me, as L believes. I know that she needs to act when anxious, is trying to be helpful.

Anyway, it strikes me, as it did L, that the obstructive force which hits the rounder and backer is quite absurdly powerful. It destroys the part which is "old and new," preventing the machine from operating. Furthermore, a "tooth" is also broken, a capacity to chew or grind, make function smoothly. This weird obstruction, L has said, must be the last gasp of the negative force and when the book finally comes out, it will be a great achievement and take the collective by storm! I know that she, too, cares for me. It is so nice to be loved by each friend in a different way! But there is also, as L has shown, a profound trickster, devil, or obstructive consciousness, shown by its powerful continuation in the collective. Better to just register that energy, move out of the way, or accept it, rather than battle it. Enjoy what one can, accept the way of serenity and peace.

I woke up this morning in my customary sad mood. Later on, L said she had a dream which reflected it. She dreamed that she was cleaning out a swimming pool with lots of gelatinous "gunk" in it. I was nearby and suffering because all my "advisors" (on the astral?) were disagreeing with each other and there was no way for them to get together because of the depth of the shadow problem. This was far deeper than Jung had worked with or realized, because all their shadows were intertwined and it was, indeed, at the level of mutual contamination and much more than an individual working and becoming conscious of his own shadow. Particularly, it was an analyst who was hindering their union. Further, I was, somehow in my writing — the first book, she thinks — trying to pass some sort of test. I was also trying to deal with this complex shadow problem. I could give up the test, perhaps, and let them all be stuck with their own dilemma.

L's dream expresses it rather well, I think. I seem to be stuck with my "tests" and with the diversity of all my "advisors," inside and out. I feel less "poisoned" this week-end, but I am sad. About the book, as usual — no word from the bindery, and D's phone is still not connected, of course. Better, but still in the swamp. There are some new calls for therapy, which is nice, since my practice has gone down, in this depression-time, and it is mostly my psyche which is hurting, not so much the body. But I don't know where to begin to work on myself, if at all. Maybe just quietly wait.

It is May 12. A week has passed since I last wrote. Things are both different and the same. They are the same in that the book is still not out, although, according to the bindery, they will be fully bound today. I also presume that the check which D gave him (at last) is good, but whether he will pick up the books today is another matter. The printer — darkened be his name — told the bindery man not to give him the books until the check has cleared the bank. He also said that he will not be in a position to make the dust-jackets until the middle of this week. I had a terrible conversation with this little rat, as my wife says he looks, on Saturday, and I am continually wondering how it is that I have been involved with such people all these months. What, Oh Lord, is the meaning of this involvement with such people? Shadow-work, I think, just as L's dream suggested.

I have practically given up the belief I proclaimed in that book: that God is becoming human in all of us and that we are astounded, uplifted and torn apart by that event. The more I see certain people, such as the printer, the less they seem divine, in any creative or impressive sense, and the more they seem like moles or rats, totally consumed with their own selves, images, desires, and so on. I, too, alas, have become one-sided and mole-like in my own blind pursuit of having my book come out. So I have to face my own shadow.

A week since writing. I have seen H since then, and am so pleased that she seems so well and free from the pain and weeping and madness of these last two years! She, too, struggles with her book(s) and I hope that hers will come out and find their way in the world easier than mine has been.

Am I a writer? ... I wonder. I saw, in yesterday's paper, that the writer of *Watership Down,* a fanciful book with great success, himself had Jungian analysis years ago and says that if one does not write and keep in touch with the inner characters in one's daily or weekly life, then they go away forever. He must know. My figures, have they gone away? Or, if not gone away, is there any interesting material they have to tell? I do not know. Edwards, I think his name is, says that one has to sit by the typewriter for hours, until the flow begins, and to do it almost every day. I sit here all right and I know whereof he speaks, having written in that way in the past. But now? I do not know. I do not know if I have the desire myself. And now that I have moved toward desire and pleasure as the mode of existence, why turn even writing into another obligation?

Some minutes later: I have been reading von Franz's *Number and Time* and find her discussion of the transition from the alchemical "three" to the "four" in psychological attitude helpful. The "three" with its spirit, certainty, and dynamism, leaves out the problem of matter, wholeness and, particularly, the shadow and darkness. I realize, just as L's dream suggested, that my struggle to get my book out, to somehow realize my Self in life, is all part of that same process, from three to four. *The Tree,* after all, had the number six as a main symbol, and this is a double three. That, I felt, arose from the problem of the Knight dream, of the Five and the One. These, given up and sacrificed, brought back six dimes or six tens. Well, now that I want to realize those six tens in life, in the world, in books, in my own spirit manifesting, then the problem of the five (as center among the four) and the one (totality, continuity, but unexpressed), still holds. My six dimes equal sixty. Within that sixty there are fifteen, even! One and five again. But this is just number play. The truth is that I have been immersed so deeply in the shadow — matter, failure, inferiority, stupidity, cupidity — for years now, that I could not see that this darkness is part of the whole. May my dreams show me a further way into this struggle!

The disintegration goes on. Yesterday I saw an old patient, who was a Miss "Something" once. Now she lives in the Bay area, but is unhappy there; it is overcrowded and not alive. Deadness. She flew down here to see me and nothing worked: plane, computer, auto rental. All is breaking down.

And my dream last night: first came the problem of a young black man who was suffering loss of meaning. In the second dream I was with a Japanese. We were climbing down an open-staired place and I was trying to hold on to both my coat and the railing. It was difficult. A dare-devil chap was on a bicycle, high up. I awakened with that sense of loss of meaning. I see, now, the need to come down to earth, deal with the shadow, as I felt yesterday upon reading von Franz's *Number and Time*.

MAY 15, 1975

The disintegration is coming to an end. Yesterday, D informed me that he was picking up the books from the bindery, that he had paid the man, had paid the printer as well, and that the latter was going to have the dust-jackets ready by Friday afternoon. Tonight I am going to D's place, to autograph books for those who ordered them this way. I shall have the finished book — not the dust jacket yet, that would be too perfect, but close enough. I shall have them in hand, ready to be sent out by next Monday. I must register this longed-for event now. My friends, Haggard, Tewfik people and Steersman, I shall talk of this with you after the "miracle" finally occurs.

It is almost two weeks since I last wrote a note. All has happened, and nothing has happened. I did get the book, as I had last noted, and on that same day, but rather than feeling elated and happy, I went into further depression. Was this a *post-partum* condition? I don't know. But it was made worse by the fact of having dinner with my erstwhile "Judge" of the past, the man who had betrayed me. It was a difficult evening for me. Not a word was said about my pain or about the betrayal. There was much talk about his illness, of course, and his children, but it was all as if nothing had happened. Perhaps for him, who has had several strokes, wears a pacemaker in his heart, and has extensive memory loss, nothing did happen that he can remember. I could not bring myself to say anything, in respect for my wife's judgment in the matter, and partly because I did not want to cause further pain either. But the effect was devastating. The next day, indeed, was a dark one for me. It was as if the two events that were to change my life, the publishing of my book and the encounter with my old analyst friend and "judge" had accomplished nothing at all!

A day or so later, however, the wheels turned. I went to a funeral during the day, that of a sister of my maternal grandmother, and visited the graves of my paternal grandfather and grandmother. That encounter with the dead somehow made me feel better. I met some members of my family, said yes, my book is out, and I started to grow cheerful. That night, I went to the fiftieth birthday party of an old friend and gave my book as a present. There were several people whom I had not seen in many years, and it was nice to have my book in hand. I was in good form and feeling very well. The next afternoon, I had my own little party with close friends and family and felt fine, indeed. But now, just two days later, I am again a bit bleak and don't know why.

I just called Henry Miller, wanting to give him a copy of the book. Am I down because I do not feel like a writer? Postpartum? Those two days of joy were really splendid! I don't know now, why my mood has changed. Cut off from myself or the unconscious? Maybe. I hear the birds, that's nice. Read? Write? Talk to Haggard? My wife gave me several of his books and a biography of him for my birthday. The Tewfik people: Do I feel their reality? ... Read a little, and see.

... I have read a bit in that charming little book, *He!*, by Robert Johnson, about the Grail legend. As I read at the outset of his psychological interpretation, he spoke of *anima* moods and their trapping character. This seems to be where I have been during these last months, at least, if not for the years since turning age forty. The mood-trapping by the unconscious continues, despite all my work in active imagination, the creativity of the stories, teaching, etc. As I read, I would tend to nod off, almost fall asleep. I would let this happen and then feel the non-verbal depth of the unconscious. An image that appeared first was that of an Asian, a Buddha-like man, rather heavy and seated, meditating. This is like an image I had on that astral-travel weekend, of a Tibetan monk meditating, but the latter had a number of faces all over his be-robed body; he had a multiple religious consciousness. These wise figures appear to me in an introverted, non-speaking way, not like the *anima.* What has happened to my friends from Tewfik Land? Are you there, my friends? Do you know of the appearance, finally, of the book?

They do not answer. I wonder if this oriental person is of Tewfik Land. I wonder if he is indeed an old-wise-man from that place. No answer. I wonder, too, if Johnson's negative view of the pursuit of happiness is correct. I have been learning from my wife and L that the enjoyment of each moment *is* the Grail and I think they may be right. The Grail King, at the end, the figure of God on earth, pays full attention to the Grail. The right question is to ask whom the Grail serves; that will heal the Fisher King. Serving God, yes. But where is God, and what does God want? Is He not within, above all, and what does He want now?

How can I ease those *anima* wounds of moods and depression? How can I make joyful the failed writer, give power to the impotent magician? No answer. Partly I enjoy the reading, as I have enjoyed looking at my own book, *The Tree: Tales in Psycho-Mythology.* Perhaps I should now be editing my sequels to *The Tree,* that is, *The Quest* and *The Love.* They need it. I hope that they will be published, too, but I shall wait and see what comes to me about writing.

"But really, Haggard and Tewfik People, are you not pleased that the book is actually out in the world? Truly on its own way? Not many copies have been printed, I know, and there is certainly no great burst of enthusiasm for it, as L anticipated, but it is walking about on its own, as wished, and as you, people of Tewfik, promised. Are you not pleased?"

I sense you nodding, though I have difficulty seeing you. But I must add my thanks to you, my thanks for your patience, your support, your assuring me of my value and worth when I could not do this for myself. I thank you from the bottom of my heart, you and those other friends from other lands of the unconscious, from Tewfik and the rest. But I thank you particularly right now, because all these last months, these months of despair when I have been with you, wondering if I could call myself a writer, you have been there for me. I still wonder if I can *continue* to call myself a writer, but you are there and I thank you, deeply.

Some days later, June 5, 1975, and I am again in the soup, confused, regarding whether this is writing, whether more needs to be said, how to proceed. I do want to write again and preferably in an easier, more fantasy-like, "literary" mode, as I used to. Is that possible? And now I want to ask my friends in Tewfik Land, Mercurius, Haggard, the Green Man and Lady of Tewfik Land, what they desire.

"What is it then, friends, that you would wish about the writing? Do you, like my friends the Knight, the Arab, and the rest, have stories to tell also?"

I see that Mercurius does not; he *is* the story, he *is* the angel, he *is* the continuity, the being, the driver and the driven. He nods his affirmation that what I say is true. And what of Haggard and the Tewfik Lady? ... Haggard seems uncertain, doubtful; he ponders. The Tewfik Lady looks at me warmly, earthily. She is silent, but I sense that she would gladly participate in a story involving alchemy or about any sensuous, physical place. Is she not, as she said, the "spirit of flesh"? Tewfik Man, blond and strong, is noncommittal. In a way, he is like the Knight himself, but a sort of Nordic version of him, if one can say so. He seems not ready to tell a story, unless I want him to.

In short, they are not eager to tell a tale, it seems. Do they merely reflect my own ambivalence? I do not know. Perhaps, if I were more eager and assertive, or devoted, then they would accommodate. The only one who seems eager to be involved is the Tewfik Lady. She would take up the alchemical process, I know. But would I? Would I be committed, say, to a weekly talk with her, weekly fantasy? Would I see it through? ... Probably I would, if it were more like the *Tree* series, limited in time. In fact, I have thought about this whole work as perhaps a variation of the *Tree,* the story of failures, many of them, paralleling those of the Tree people.

But what do I want right now? And what do they want? I lean toward further editing of *The Quest* tales but I'm also drawn to just enjoy life. Yet I want to be deeply involved in writing once more, knowing it as I once did. That immersion, supposed to occur at the end of '72 or '74, did not happen. I think that I must now ask for a dream for inspiration.

Please unconscious, and please God, tell me of your general tenor. I would like my work to take a more "story" form, since the "personal" has gone about as far as I can take it. I am not even certain that I can "clean it up" in such a fashion as to make it "storyable." But I think that this could be accomplished and am ready to go on.

It feels as if the Failed Alchemist is there, ready to engage the Tewfik Lady, but on other grounds, or names. Not as an Artist, perhaps, who sees her as Muse, but as an Alchemist, who sees her as Mystical Sister. I start to feel some excitement with that. As if the Artist ends up with the Muse and the Alchemist with the Mystical Sister and they meet in Tewfik Land or elsewhere. The Healer and others also meet there, encountering the same person. Mercurius, for example, is Steersman for the Artist and Angel for the Healer. Perhaps the meeting is of Mercurius and Muse, Angel and Mystical Sister, coming together.

All right. I am ready. I want a structure in which to pour fantasy, creativity, meaning, and being. I want all those "tendencies" of the Hungry Ghost, of the Son of the Arab, etc., to find a place. Gee, Hungry Ghost could be of the Failed Buddhist! He did not achieve satori, he failed in Self-Realization! In other words, I would write many stories again as in the first tales. All that struggle about editing of the series could be deferred for a time. I could take them one at a time, or as a series. Who are they?

Unhealed Healer (body healing)
Unhealed Healer (spirit healing, among Gods)
> or maybe both are one (very long tale, too long).
Failed Artist (Haggard et al, adventures in Tewfik Land).
Failed Magician (not clear, but involved with occult)
Untransformed Alchemist (with Lady of Tewfik).

That is six already. I should change names, but there is certainly ample material for a trilogy: The Losers or The Failures. And this is made possible, of course, because all of the Tree people made it, are no longer failures! The next step is to get on with writing just as it comes. Sorting can come later. But the reportage, what shall I do about that? That can be edited out later also. O.K. Shall I use different books or continue in one? Please Haggard, or friends from the unconscious, I need an answer and some help. Please come tonight or before the weekend and answer. I beg of you.

Days later: they do not come.

## JUNE 18, 1975

I feel stuck as a writer. Yesterday, a Japanese person, reading my book, did not think that the Ronin I wrote about in *The Tree* was very Japanese. This hurt. Also, in doing the editing for the second part of *The Quest*, Mother and Daughter, I felt that the writing was not as good as the first part — the "tasks" of the Demeter-Persephone myth got resolved too easily. Yet it all turned out fine and I think it will be O.K. But still, the issue is that I seem to be continually uncertain about how to proceed in my writing.

There is the continuing hassle about the various figures or about what to include where. Right now, there is also an unfrocked Priest. But, more fundamentally, is there a Writer?

"Haggard, my friend, are you still there? Have you patiently waited for me? Is our work finished?"

"Not finished, Marvin, hardly started."

"Where would you go with it? What is your wish?"

"My wish, like yours, is to produce something of merit."

"Yes, of course. But I wonder where or how to do it. Should we continue, you and I and the Steersman, in Tewfik Land, perhaps with the Lady thereof? Or should we voyage anew? You are a good writer, where would you like to go?"

"I have no wishes right now, none. Quietly contented."

"What about the wish to 'produce something of merit'?"

"Yes, that is always there. But it has no focus now."

"All right. But what do you think of my getting hurt so easily, of the 'failure' of the Ronin story and of the possible superficiality of the mother-daughter tale?"

"No, no, no! You are too hard on yourself! Naturally, it is disappointing that the Japanese chap should not see the Japanese tale as you wish it. But that is his failing more than yours. You are writing — have written — a tale in relation to a myth-process. His consciousness cannot take in all of that. As he said, he found some of the tales too difficult, with strange symbolism. As for the other, it is perfectly fine. Do not put down your work because you are in a quiet place just now. Do not do that. Continue, you are just fine! I support you.

"Thank you, Haggard. I feel better talking with you."

JUNE 20, 1975

Days later. I sit now before this typewriter, eager and fearful. I am eager to write, to express, to convey, to fulfill my own wild dreams of being a good writer, and fearful that I cannot accomplish it. I am feeling awfully good at the moment as a therapist, in that I am working effectively and deeply, yet also very much being my Self in all its complexity, reactivity and spontaneity. The two groups of professional therapists that I lead are doing well, and I find my individual therapy has improved and deepened over the last weeks.

I am grateful for the influx of energy and love that I feel, coming from God, coming from the Self, validating me and what I am doing. Yet the very act of writing about these things now is puzzling to me. This is strange — not because it is positive and appreciative, for I am glad of that — but because I never know if I am really a writer or am writing anything valuable. I don't know even, if in this latest series since 1971, there is one story, several stories or many, several healers and writers and priests, or what? If many, what goes where? At the moment, I am solving this by merely writing, not even putting a date on it, but just writing now as I feel and want to write. But this is not active imagination, it is not, as B writes — thoughts about therapy, for example — it is more like a statement of where I am. Yet it too has felt stilted — when I merely report and am not living in the moment of writing. Yes, living in the moment, even in writing, that seems important. Not to plan too much and to take relation-ships and matters just as they present themselves. Yet structure seems necessary. It is perhaps the perennial struggle in me between Jupiter expanding, leading and benevolent, and Saturn constricting, limiting and planning for the future. When I know that these are squared in my horoscope, in fundamental differ-ence, that Jupiter rules my mid-heaven (I am meant to be a leader, to be expansive) and that Saturn sits with my Moon in Scorpio, I know an old pain and a conflict. Judgment, the depressing character of Saturn, sits on the feminine and feelings, and these are in the 7th House of partnership and relationship. For me relationship with the Self is like that with other people. Indeed, I think that my Priest story should probably take that up, since his alchemical relationship failed.

So, here I am, expressing how it is and asking now, what the Self wants in this, in my writing? Does the Self want me to do what I am doing? I think so, since I feel a little relieved, a little less tense — or does it want a story or both? Self, where art thou, say I, as some Juliet longing for Romeo. Yes, my soul longs for its lover, just as my new patient does. She paints pictures for herself which become art and writes poems, too. Well, then? Now I stop. Nothing more to say ... Self? Self?

For answer I see a little mouse, like the rat I fished out of the pool the other day and saved from drowning, but not because I wanted to save it. I just wanted to get it out of the pool. But I saved it anyhow and threw the squirming thing over the fence. But this is a little mouse, with big eyes to be sure, but small in the rest of him. I at once think that this may be the Self coming to me in little, frightened form. O.K. My problem may be expan-siveness, inflation, and I need the littleness, the fear of the mouse, as compensation. What does the mouse say?

Nothing. But H. Rider Haggard is also there now, and I think that he has something to say about it. Do you, Rider?

"I do. Look at yon mouse. Delicate, soft. Look at him. Could you describe him? Could you point out the special grayness of his skin and fur? The special delicacy of his whiskers as they wiggle there, from side to side? The special softness in those eyes? Could you just observe and record? Rather than quickly engage in dialogue and adventure?"

"I could, I suppose, Haggard, but that is not my style usually. I am not a good writer of scenes or facts. Besides, I think that you were an adventurous type of writer, in contrast with descriptive or reflective, were you not?"

"Yes, of course. But I am suggesting now that you add 'matter' in your writing, to bring it down a bit. Less heroic, perhaps (but still heroic in adventure or grandeur), but more contained, less quick and facile. Weren't you, after all, complaining the other day that your own Mother and Daughter story was too quick and easy in solutions?"

"I was, it is true. I wonder if that would give it the needed substance and quality. My starting of the Unfrocked Priest story was fine without all that."

"True."

"But I am quick again, Haggard. Already I am thinking about these writings as another story! 'Conversations with a Writer' or many writers even! It must be Mercurius, the Steersman, sending these rapid, inflating directions, ideas and intuitions which do not seem to hold up or carry weight."

I now see Haggard grinning. Mercurius, the dark Steersman, is also grinning broadly. We all know that what I said is true, that the Steersman is the author of this. Immediately I think of all the figures being part of my horoscope and that the Judge is Saturn, the expansive benevolent is Jupiter, that Venus and the Moon are other parts of me, etc. So even as I realize that Mercurius is running the show, he runs it some more by suggesting that many others are present. Enough! And enough of my Gemini Sun!

Let me get back to the mouse, as Haggard suggests. After all, I asked for the Self, the image of God in my own psyche, and I got a mouse! The mouse, too, is quick and clever, I think. Haggard says describe it, calm down by description and other such sensation-function activity. That is one good answer to the Steersman's quick and automatic intuitions. But what about feeling and relationship? That is Aphrodite perhaps or Venus, seen astrologically, just as Jupiter might be my thinking function (or is it in the Judge of Saturn?). All that is merely a possibility which leads nowhere! All right. Back then to the mouse. I shall speak to it. Feeling is my way to link up in relationship after all.

"So, Sir Mouse, as representative of the Self, at this moment, or the Self itself, can you, will you, speak to me?"

The mouse then does two things, just as the Self so frequently does, expressing its binary quality, I suppose. The mouse does not answer at all at first, merely wiggling its nose like a rabbit, and then it speaks very deeply in a bass voice, quite unexpectedly. All right, I can see that this is the Self as animal, unspeaking, deep in the body and instinct, yet also the human Self, paradoxically powerfully spoken. "Smaller than small and bigger than big" like Purusha. All right. What does the mouse say?

It makes a single deep sound as if chanting. Then I hear the sounds of the Buddhist mantra, *Om Mani Padme Hum.* It chants and chants. Now I see a series of Asian monks, dressed in yellow robes, chanting also. They chant the name of the Jewel in the Lotus, calling out the name of God. But Buddhists don't call it God. We Jews do that! Still, that is what it is. But why does the mouse chant in a Buddhist manner and is then replaced by the vision of a group of monks, Tibetan I think, also chanting? I listen and am still. Haggard joins me in a respectful attitude toward this mouse and these monks, but the Steersman stands quietly in our boat, holding an oar, merely looking at what is going on. He is stilled at the moment (but he smiles as I say this).

So we listen, Haggard and I, to the sounds of the chanting. I like the sounds, but grow weary and sleepy. At last I want to fall asleep with such a pleasant sound and the vision of high mountains and blue sky, with the monks chanting in clear, pure air. Sleep seems fine and in this the Mouse level of God is also satisfied. It now licks me and closes its eyes, too. The monks chant us a lullaby of the Lord, Buddha's jewel in the lotus, then grow still. As do I.

JULY 22, 1795

It has been a month since I have attended to these pages of the *Unpublished Writer,* but it seems even longer for me. Various things have happened, some good and some bad, and I want to report them. Not that I feel much like a writer just now, but I do want to continue my "reportage" and to keep up with this attempt of mine to redeem myself as a writer.

The good thing that has happened is that I have been interviewed about my book. A man who has a regular program on a radio station (public, non-commercial, of course), came to me in another connection and I told him about my book. He was interested in interviewing me for this program and he did so. He did his own editing and I did not know how it would come out. Well, I heard the program the other day and I must say that I was very pleased. I have been on the radio now and then over the years, being interviewed about one thing or another, but never in connection with my own writing. This time it was so, and there was a most noticeable difference for me. I loved it! I was not arrogant, nor unrelated, nor did I speak too fast, nor was I without humor. Rather, I was true to my spirit but open to the man, firm about my views but non-dogmatic. I even spoke about writing my book of failures! In all, I was well pleased. I was myself and it seemed all right. What a thing for me to say after all these years! What a triumph, at last, of acceptance of Self! I, who continually judge and find fault with myself, at last find it all right. The Judge is satisfied. Well then, I wonder what Haggard and my friends think about that?

"Haggard? Haggard, are you there?"

"I am here at your service, where you left me."

"Yes, how nice. Although I am still awaiting the arrival of your book, *Wisdom's Daughter,* as you promised, but it still has not appeared. It makes me wonder if it is indeed you to whom I speak or a creation in my own psyche."

"It is I. *Wisdom's Daughter* will arrive in due course, as I promised. But not just yet. I do not know exactly when. We dead are not all that omniscient, as you know very well, but it will arrive. I have set certain things in motion."

"Good, I am glad! Do you know about the interview and about that damn publisher whose phone is still out of order?"

"Yes, I know."

"Do you know that I brought the book myself to a bookstore and contacted another? That I got fifty of the bloody things from the publisher to sell myself, and I have already sold twenty of them?"

"Yes, I know that, also. Good for you. I had always had a hard time with publishers, despite what people said, and I always had the thought that I might do better on my own."

"But I find it a nuisance. I wish to hell that I had a proper publisher who would at least get the book out to bookstores and handle all the business part. At least I would know then, that my child was having decent care."

"Naturally."

"But also some people have loved my book and a lady called after hearing me on the radio, desperately wanting a copy. A German lady, a writer herself, wanted the book and was not able to find the publisher! I gave her and her bookstore the address of the publisher, and I know that he will at least send out a book! But how the hell are people going to find his address if he has no phone?"

"Trust, Marvin, trust."

"O.K. I will ... I'll be back with you in a day or so. Thank you for your support, Rider, I appreciate it!"

"You're welcome. It is my pleasure, and I must remind you, I have a stake in this as well!"

JULY 28, 1975

"I am quite blue again, Haggard, my friend. Walking in Westwood the other night, where all the students are, I wandered into several bookstores, none of which carried my book ... No word at all from that out-of-contact publisher ... Imagine, a publisher who has no telephone, cannot be reached by people who want to buy a book! I have now sold over twenty books myself in less than a month. I do better than he! But, it is sad that the book does not even find a place to walk around in the world. Then there are my two sequels, *The Quest* and *The Love,* without a sign of a publisher, to say nothing of my Failure book, really a failure!

There have been a couple of nice events, though. For one, my father came to me yesterday and wanted to buy a book for a customer of his who is married to a girl I loved in the second grade. She, having heard about the book, wanted a copy inscribed to her. I was glad to do this, recalling our days in elementary school. And then I got a letter from Henry Miller. I had sent him a copy of a Jerusalem Post article about Isaac Bashevis Singer, whom Miller likes very much, and I told him too about my work on failure. I told him I was trying to work my way out of it. Here is what he said:

"I am most interested in your series, 'The Failures'. My beloved subject! Why 'work your way out of it?' Isn't it a rather blessed state? Let me see a chapter or two some time!"

That is a nice remark and I think that he means it. He certainly lived a long time with failure! But then he also experienced a lot of success. I could use a bit of that too.

So, Haggard, that is where I am. Except that yesterday, in my blueness, I picked up a book of yours that my wife bought for me at my last birthday, *The Yellow God*. I got more than halfway through it in a couple of hours. It was you, all right, your "characters": the fine English gentleman, the scoundrels, the helpful black, the hint at the forthcoming *anima* there in the jungle plus, of course, the excellent lady at home, waiting. This came out in 1908, when you were about 52 ...

I interrupt. A bookstore in Westwood, where I wandered the other night, just phoned. The manager reading my note asking if they would order my book, just called and said that they had ordered several as much as a year ago and had never received any. Well, the book is out a couple of months after all, but he is so irresponsible that he did not even respond. I call back the nice lady manager, explained and hope that she would re-order. She will.

"Oh, Rider, what a drag! Even when the 'Unpublished Writer' is published, he is not really 'out there'! ... You laugh. Do you find that humorous?"

"I do, Marvin, I do. I think that your friend Henry Miller is right. To be a failure is a blessing, even if it does not seem so now. At least one is out of the harmful limelight and can proceed about one's business. That is the main thing. Anyway, you will not be much of a failure, as we have already said. Enough, though. How do you like my book?"

"I like it. It is you, all right: exciting, good plot, lots of action. But the characters are pretty one-sided, are they not? And do I detect a fair amount of British arrogance? Fair play and all that is very well, but to glorify the fine British gentlemen and to mock and show prejudice toward Jews, Blacks, Frenchmen, well, that is a bit much, isn't it?"

"Yes, it is. You are right. But, in my day, well ... that was the going thing, wasn't it? We had the White Man's Burden and all.

My prejudice was not as great as that of the average British gentleman after all."

"I imagine not. I have your biography here, also given me by my wife, but have not started to read it yet, thinking that perhaps you would tell me more about yourself without that additional information. Besides, there is a sort of 'test,' isn't there, about our relationship? Whether it is really 'you' or not? Whether there is a 'Haggard' in my head, different from the true spirit?"

"Yes, I know. That is fine with me. Either way. As long as we continue this joint project for a time. It is of value for me, as I have said, to keep contact with a living writer. There are things that I need to know and experience also, and I cannot do it alone here in the Land of the Dead."

"What is it really, that you wish to know, Rider?"

"What I want to know, Marvin, is how that scintilla or spark of consciousness can unite with matter in that very special way to produce creativity or life or soul — as you call it. It is the Muse that interests me in her real form. Not just that archetypal idea of Jung's, which I appreciate and which touches me particularly since he liked my work, but the Muse herself. I have said that to you before, but perhaps I have not been so clear. I am not so clear myself. If you were to read my life story, you would understand better. I was a man of action as well as reflection, of reality as well as fantasy. Behind it all was the quality, the capacity, the feminine driving force, if you will — mirrored, for example, in *She!* — which spoke of a union of the two worlds. Now that I am dead, I am even more appreciative of this dilemma. I would like, indeed, to advance my consciousness and appreciation of this problematic union, focused in the Muse, so that whatever I may experience on earth or otherwise in the future, I will be centered in a new way."

"I am not sure that I understand you entirely, Haggard. I am not even sure that your words are coming through to me in an accurate way. I understand, somehow, the problem of the union of the scintilla with matter, spirit and flesh. I understand, too, your pre-occupation with the Muse — kind of, but not entirely. Let me tell you a dream I had the other night. It occurs to me that it may be related to what you are concerned with.

"In this dream, I find myself at a seacoast. It is late evening and the sun has recently set. I am there with just a few people and we are gazing, enraptured, at a huge, full moon, which is covering the sky before us, many times larger than the usual one. Has it come so much closer to the earth, so that now it is only a few thousand miles away? We are struck with its intense light. All the shadows of its mountains and craters are readily apparent. As we watch, there fall from this fantastic Moon many bits of wood which are like driftwood. They fall to the sea and to the beach in great quantities. People start to pick them up. Now many others come to the beach to gaze at this wondrous sight. My wife is now with me too. Among the people who come are a father and his teenage son. The man, ruddy-faced, seems to know me and I greet him, but he does not return the greeting. The driftwood now falls in greater quantity and I am concerned that the people might get hurt. Two huge driftwood trees fall onto the beach in the midst of the crowd, but luckily no one is hurt. I am aware of the fine gray color of the wood, its smooth and glossy surface, as if it were polished by the sea, and I wonder that such a thing can fall from the Moon. End of dream.

"This dream, Rider, seems to be one of those 'other-worldly' dreams, does it not? Of the same sort that underlie *She!* and some of Quartermain's experiences, don't you think? The Moon was the anciently believed land of the dead. Even though our astronauts have landed upon it, it still is no mere dry bit of meteorite with sand, but is a numinous lamp aglow with a strange life. And here closer now to earth is this satellite, symbol of a feminine presence, Rider, close to your Muse, I think. This falling of debris from there to here, driftwood from old, dead trees, is this, at last, some message that my own poor book, *The Tree,* dies hardly after being born? Devoid of proper parenting, does it collapse and pour out its feeble remnants (the few extant copies)? But no; why would it be in that form? Something else is being said to me. As I say this, I feel dizzy and ill. The message, whatever it is, is not being assimilated. I am too much in my head and my nervous system is nauseous. So be it ... What do you think, Haggard? What does the dream mean to you?"

"I am no psychologist nor interpreter of dreams of others or my own. But I do sense the flavor of the dream, its atmosphere and quality. The light, the grayness, the unusual events, all that does touch me. But I can say no more."

"Well, Haggard, I can't say much either. I had a dream long ago, in which I held a trunk of a tree, filled with explosives, and carried it when all others ran. I was told to hold it. It exploded, but I survived. I have dreamed, too, as you know, of being initiated by branches of a tree. And, at last, I have written a book called *The Tree* and have studied the Tree of Life, the Kabbalistic method of the inner energies. But in the dream these are dead or remnants ... I do not understand ... What do I do when I do not understand a dream? I continue the dream in my fantasy and put myself into it. Would you like to accompany me in this, Rider?"

"I would, indeed. Should we not ask our Steersman also? He has accompanied us to Tewfik Land, he could surely be of use to us in relation to a moonscape."

"Yes, indeed. Come with me, both of you ..."

I find myself on that beach, watching the fall of the driftwood, but instead of standing there, I am in the air moving toward this moon, as if I were myself a spaceship or engaged in astral travel. I move in this fashion, weightless. But where are Haggard and the Steersman? They are not with me. They stand outside, but are perfectly capable of watching me as I move, and ... being there as I land. For I do land on this Moon, which is just as the pictures show. I can breathe however and I therefore know that it is another kind of Moon or that my non-physical body does not require oxygen on this Moon. I see no trace of trees, driftwood, or anything.

I sit down on the sandy surface. I look to Earth, which is huge in front of me. I focus upon that beach where the driftwood is falling. It now covers the area, but falls no more. It is quiet, empty. No one is there. Nor is there anyone here either. I am alone. I sense the presence of Haggard and the Steersman, there is a consciousness of them at hand, but I am alone. As if I am the last man on Earth, but I am on the Moon, and I know it is not so. It is only my own aloneness that I feel. Aloneness and failure. Quiet. Illusion. I breathe. I sink more deeply into the sand. I feel oppressed, depressed. Some jazz music plays in the background as I sit, also at my typewriter. I am in a hot room, hearing a neighbor play jazz, and I am alone on the Moon, sitting in a sandpile. And now at the thought of the sandpile I start to giggle. Absurd, meaningless. Laughter comes and with it objectivity, at least a little. The lonely Failure and the second childhood of an old man sitting in a sandpile. I throw sand upon myself, half way between agitation and play. I breathe. Lord? Lord? ... No answer.

Now Haggard has joined me and squats beside me. The Steersman joins us too, black and handsome. We are quiet. I have a sense of living in that in-between moment that Haggard hinted at: between the scintilla of consciousness and the concreteness of life. Here I am, sitting before a typewriter in a house without air-conditioning on a hot summer day; and here I am, sitting on the sand of the Moon with a dead writer and an archetypal spirit. It is both absurd and real: I am depressed, full of illusion, and objective — between the two worlds and in them both. Creation, said Haggard, is related to this state, and I suppose he is right. Here suspended and living in two worlds, there is a basis for creation and new life. In the midst of falling debris and decay of the old, is there only nothingness and absurdity, or is creation possible? Which shall it be?

The three of us sit there: I with sand on me like a child, Haggard squatting, the Steersman strong and erect. I am like a child, like Haggard, the concerned father, and like the Steersman, an eternal spirit and hero. I now understand another fragment of the dream, the father and son. Ruddy-faced father and son do not know me, but I know now: Father (Haggard) - Son (myself) and Holy Spirit (Steersman), these survive in the two worlds. Real-not real, absurd-meaningful, poised in-between. Shall there be creation? Or shall there be nothingness? Which shall it be, Haggard? Which shall it be, Steersman? Which shall it be, God?

For answer, there came the air-conditioning man! Fresh air, my friends, just ask for new spirit and there it comes! This world between the worlds, between the world of the living and the dead, the spirit and the flesh, fantasy and reality: it is, indeed, a curious place and one that I can see strongly interests Haggard. He, a dead writer, I, a living one, engaged in some transfer between the two worlds. But it is more than a transfer, it is a problem, the same as spirit and flesh, or creation and nothingness.

Enough now. As I sit, a child upon the moon in my sandpile, a disillusioned and failed writer upon the earth at my typewriter, talking to a dead writer and a Mercurial spirit, pretending to be engaged in writing a book about failure! ... Laughter. It is not madness because madness would choose: this world or the other. And yet I have worked with the mad who straddled both worlds; I remember one who found meaningful messages from license plate numbers!

"All right, Haggard. Say something helpful, please, or you Steersman, Mercurial One, say something please!"

"The Lord is my Shepherd ..." laughs Mercurius Steersman.

"My shepherd is the Lord ..." continues Haggard.

And I know that I am no sheep, but a tormented, worried, slightly mad writer. I know that the famous writer, Henry Miller, wants to hear about my failures, and I think that if I go and read to him the first part of this series, about meeting Haggard and all, that he would be amused.

"But Rider, is that what this is all about? Is that what life is about? An amused absurdity? I think not. Nor do I believe that you think so. One can not lead a meaningless life very long."

Haggard nods. Steersman, too. I flee from the great sandpile of the Moon, the place of the dead, and rush posthaste back to Tewfik Land, where the Orange Lady lives, where the Muse dwells in the background, where there is life and love and something more of meaning than this dead Land of the Moon which drops its dead life upon the earth. Now I am once more with the Orange Lady who touches me. She laughs gently, as I feel her body and hear her breathing.

"Is life so precious that half-life, subtle life, is better than dead life?" she asks. And I know that she is speaking of her own land, in contrast to the Moon-Land. I nod feebly knowing that this is true. And knowing also that sometimes half-life is better than full-life, and she laughs aloud. But it is not a cruel laugh, nor without feeling, but like the last laughs of my friends, Haggard and Steersman. For they too now live a half-life, a matterless life, which flows but carries no weight without these fingers, this typewriter, this breathing, this sound of a now humming air-conditioner. It is this too that interests them.

... I just called the public relations man at Pickwick bookstore, who was going to do something about displaying my book. He went on vacation today, I am told, for two weeks, and no one knows about my book! Well, Henry Miller, how is that for Failure? Blessed is it? I also called the Bodhi Tree Bookstore, where six of my books were supposed to have been sent. None are there, no one has ever heard of it. Blessed is it, Henry Miller? Blessed perhaps compared to being dead altogether! Why then hold onto life so much, when there is such illusion and disappointment and defeat. What do you say, Haggard? Or Steersman? Or Orange Lady? Is there anything?

"Only defeat," repeats Haggard, and he looks sad. "The only defeat that I know of, is death. That is a final one. But even that is not so final!"

"And I," says the Steersman, "know of neither. Death is no end nor is defeat. Heroes are defeated, it must needs be so. But despair and agitation? Not necessarily part of it."

"What you say is true, Haggard and Steersman," say I, as I breathe a little. "It is true. How I take defeat, my agitation and despair at the frustration is what the issue is, of course. But I seem not to be able to overcome these."

"Sh, still," says the Orange Lady, and I am strangely less agitated, still. There are no answers but irrationally my despair is alleviated and agitation is gone.

Now, a person calls who loves my book, wants to buy two more for friends. I would be almost better off selling the book myself here! Enough of my vanity and pre-occupation!

## AUGUST 6, 1975

So blue am I — for a change. A mere nothing could bring it on: a telephone call to Hunter's Book Store, to the manager who was going to look over my book and phone me back, but did not. At last I reach him and he says, simply, that the book is not "commercial." How I remember hearing that before, several years ago, when I was trying to get it published! And how it is still so, among the "commercials" of this world. That has the power to throw me into despair even yet. Not because their judgment is true or false — they certainly seem to be right — but because the very act of judgment precludes the possibility of my work finding its own non-terribly-commercial place in the world!

"Oh, Haggard! I am so low, so sad! I am such a pained, defeated, failed writer! That publisher sits in his own little hovel, does nothing, and my book has no life. And I, trying to do some of his work when he does not, meet with even more failure! I sigh. I think of you, Haggard, and your success. I think with pleasure about your book, *The Yellow God,* which I read with joy and appreciation ... You have the capacity to bring me back to my adolescence, those days of mystery and wonder, my urge to be a writer ... I start to weep. I weep for my dashed expectancies, for my repeated failures in wanting to be that "writer." I weep for the pain of many people I have known. I weep for other failed writers.

"Haggard, you are dead now, living in that in-between-world of the Dead. You say that you do not know so much about things, but perhaps you do know about life and its meaning. Perhaps you could say something soothing to me. I have become a non-heroic, weak, needy person, one who needs hugs and pats and soothing words. No more the rough hero, the proud Knight; no more the "rock" as they used to call me ... I feel sick, nauseated, my neck is stiff and I ache ... I breathe, trying to relax ... Haggard? Haggard?"

"I am here, Marvin. I am here. I know what you feel. You have felt this before. And so have I. I know that you thought of me only as a 'success,' but it is not so. So often I felt the failure. So often. Did not that scholar from Israel write to you complaining about the reception of his book? Falling between the two stools of critics? ... Writers feel that. Not recognized. Defeated. If they have a critical success, they miss the popular. And if the popular success is forthcoming — as it was with me — then the critics and scholars scoff. That is so painful ... But I know that this does not help. You need concrete help to make things better for you, a publisher who would continue to bring out your work and see that it gets a hearing. I at least had that easily. But what is that sickness of yours? Is it unwept tears?"

"I don't know. I know only frustration. Yesterday, I talked with a lady, another writer whose book was out, even a paperback edition, but she is equally pained and disappointed at the lack of publicity for her book, her inability to get her friends at the newspaper to review it. She is as chagrined as I! ... I don't know."

"Give up," says Haggard, and I am startled.

"Do you mean that, Rider? Are you telling me to give up my hopes, give up being a writer?"

"No. Just surrender. Give in. Realize that you, with your ego, your powers, whatever you have, can not bring about what you

want, what even God and the Muse have promised you.
Surrender. Let the Muse do it!"

"The Muse? You spoke of her the other day, as the union of
the scintilla of consciousness with the bit of matter that can produce creativity. She ... Yes, I know, *She!* And She was a terrible
creature in your writing, capable of endless rebirth and creativity,
but terrible in her wrath, her desires. Yet she loved you or the
Kallikrates that was the spirit of you, perhaps."

Now Haggard is silent. He will say nothing more about *She!*
or about the Muse, and I sigh once more. There is no answer, just
now, neither from me nor from him. Just sighs.

AUGUST 12, 1975

It goes on, the defeat. Yesterday, I received a phone call from the
lady who heard me interviewed on the radio, who was so eager
to get my book. She now tells me that her efforts and those of her
bookseller to get the book from the publisher have come to
nothing. He does not respond, does nothing. So now the man
does not even respond to those who want to buy the book! Not
only does he ignore the bookstores, but even individual orders!
That has thrown me once more. How can I deal with this? Try to
get the books away? See him? I suppose the latter tack should be
first, as my wife suggests. Prod him and see if there is any word
at all regarding the book from his vaunted agent, book club, or
distributors.

But I did have a dream last night, which seemed to comment
on my need for fame and success. In this dream I was living in
both the present and at the same time in the late forties and early
fifties, when I was in my early twenties. I was visiting a community in a kind of Marina, where the wealthy and successful folks
lived. I did not feel comfortable, since I do not particularly like
the sort of people I have glimpsed there on my bicycle trips or in
the restaurants at such places, but it was all right. Then I saw a
boat, which felt more comfortable, and I was on it. I could at
least connect with my own sailor experience. Now I saw a group
of men — the scene had shifted to a small restaurant-bar —
some of whom I recognized. They were successful men whom I
had known in my early twenties, but who had gained some fame
in their fields only in the last ten years or so. I was going to say

hello but felt that they would not particularly want to see me. They looked neat, youthful, successful, and I did not feel so myself. One of them had published several books and he seemed the most self-assured.

I awakened from the dream rather sad and blue. It seemed to underline my lack of success in the world. But I thought who wants that world of the Marina? Not I! What then is the dream saying? That success in that form would not be worthwhile for me? That the very life of "success," although attractive, has its shallowness, its lack of nourishment, too? I suppose so. I also thought that I must surrender this ego-place more deeply, this demand for the fulfillment of my dream and yearnings. Only when I am content, quiet, and less demanding or dependent upon success and recognition, only then will it come. But I have been in this "space" so many times! Even the "sacrifice" for the sake of later success seems equally shallow, rather like the Roman attitude toward the Gods — *do ut des,* "I give that Thou givest." No, my writing came from God(s), was the will of the God(s). But still, there is the problem of surrender or acceptance that I have not yet come to. Such an old story in itself.

"Rider, are you there? Hearing my perennial complaint?"

"I am."

"Have you something to say?"

"I do not."

"Last time we chatted, a few days ago, you suggested that I give up altogether. That I forego even the hope of success, even though you earlier assured me that things would turn out alright. I do not know what you think now."

"I think nothing. I believe that what is called for now is feeling. What you need, aside from finding that adequate publisher — the one who will appreciate your work, provide a place for your spirit on the printed page — is some compassion and empathy, my friend, which you have from me."

"Thank you Rider, I do feel that from you, as I do from no other. But I wonder if I must, as you hinted, give up all hope, stop anticipating or trying, and just enjoy the writing itself. I wonder if I should not surrender, as you say."

"I do not know. Give up, I said, and I meant it. Give up the struggle for success, since it is so painful. That is all that I meant. I did not mean more by it. For who amongst us who write can truly and freely give up the need for an outlet for his work? Not possible. But one can give up the gnawing need for success. That, yes."

"I do not know if I can do this. Tewfik Land's honor, fine; friends' and some colleagues' appreciation, very good; even your support, most excellent; but ... can I truly surrender? Even my body is rather tough in this!"

"I know what you are referring to."

"Ego, ego ... But perhaps I should just wait and see if it is like going to an Eastern land, like Tibet, to find a way to surrender this need for 'success' in the world."

Haggard is silent now, as am I.

### AUGUST 13, 1975

I saw the publisher, D, this morning, and he was all smiles. Everything is just fine, he says. Several more people have ordered the book, one professor at Columbia wants an examination copy and all the radio and TV stations should be contacting me soon. But why are not books in the stores, I ask? Well, those that order do get it. But the lady who called me after my interview says not. She says that her bookseller tried and tried, but no answer. Now the publisher shows me the books he is sending out, and that he does answer. He is hopeful of the future, the agent, book clubs.

At his place there is a tall young man with whom the publisher has just brought out a photography book. The young man has taken the pictures and D has written the commentary. The young man, no doubt, has paid for this. Anyway he seems pleasant and I don't know whether to pity him or not. I come away from the encounter and feel less down, less horrified. I suppose not all is hopeless. Perhaps the book clubs do exist, the agent exists, the TV and radio stations are not just illusion. Perhaps, when the astrological time improves in September, all will be redeemed. It is amazing how I can still hope, is it not? Let me hope for the photographer, too, or is he doomed to experience what I did?

SEPTEMBER 17, 1975

I have just come back from trying to see the publisher. I wanted to get some more books to sell (having already sold about fifty on my own), and also to get news about what is happening. He was not there. Disappointing but not devastating. I noted that I was regaining a certain composure, a capacity to withstand these disappointments. That gladdens me. I want to find another publisher for the next books of the series, but have still not given up on *The Tree* either. So whatever failure I am, I am not wiped out by it anymore! Thanks to God for that.

SEPTEMBER 26, 1975

Yesterday it looked like the whole illusion was up. I heard from A, the friend of D, that the latter is very ill, is retreating from everyone and is unable to perform at all. She was going to get back her books from him and suggested that I do the same. Well, it was hard to take in, but true. What remained was the way to do this without getting into a lot of legal tangles and unnecessary pain for him also. I talked with the lawyer who suggested that I tell D that I would like to carry more of the load, since he was sick, and get as many books as possible from him gradually over the weeks. One could also write letters to the printer, who has the master plates, and the company who presumably has the paper, to hold them for us.

Well, I found out where D was, finally reaching him at his friend's house. He said that nothing was happening, but agreed for me to take over a couple of hundred books. I also said that I would like the telephone number of the agent in New York. I felt disappointed and disillusioned, but not powerless and trapped as I did before. I could at least act in my own behalf, try to sell the books here and there and even get a new publisher or distributor. Furthermore the Jung library called me and wanted twenty books and even agreed to a suggestion that I give a talk about my work to their library meeting (he had proposed another talk about other books with other Jungians, to which I said "later"). So I felt a part of the process.

This morning I called the Jung library man. He told me that he had stopped by D's last night, got twenty books and left a check! That was supposed to be good, but naturally I was chagrined, since the money should have come to me! D already owes me five thousand dollars at least! I asked him to hold the check until I saw D on Saturday, explaining that from now on I would carry my books.

So there it is. Saturday begins my "divorce," although the lawyer and new contract were already the onset, I suppose. I hope that I can continue the transition in a reasonable way. Back to finding a distributor or publisher for it and for the other books. Well, Uranus in Scorpio, I do wish you would hurry your changes and bring me a positive outcome!

## SEPTEMBER 29, 1975

It feels as if all my "people" are depressed now. The Writer, of course, is so because of the continuing struggle with the publisher, with trying to get my work out and published, but also with a sense of futility, of there being no use in trying to write anymore. The work with Haggard seems to have stopped, all is illusion.

The only dream I can recall is one from the other night: of entering a barren room which turned out to have trees in it, perhaps even leading to a forest. But is this, too, illusion? So much illusion these years! Yes, there are threads of progress and hope: with the Jung library buying my books, leading to a talk about my work. And I am going to give a lecture in Oregon, be a keynote speaker no less. But I am invited there because of my friendship with Jim, just as John invited me to Notre Dame, not on merit alone or because of my book. So I am down. Where shall I begin? With the "downness" itself, perhaps, as in the old days? Yes.

I see myself in the forest of the dream, like that of the Knight, sitting on a stump. I sit there weeping but without tears. The forest, though, makes me feel a bit better already. At least I am in the familiar and nourishing place of the unconscious, where image and reality do come together. When I am in a "real" forest, e.g., the Sierra, I also feel marvelous. As I sit here, I think about the writing. Perhaps all my "people" come together now, all depressed, yet together. Perhaps this is where they re-unite. But what of the original separation? And what about the writing which was to work with that problem? I feel like I did when I wrote the original Knight story, needing to bring the parts of God together, to be with the "Self" and whole. But I can not do that, neither as a writer nor as anything else.

So I sit in the forest, just as the Knight did. It feels as if the many roles and parts are here with me, and all fall asleep. It is not the many parts of God that need uniting now, but the many parts of me. And I await my Angel, the one who came to the Knight. I think about the Ladies, with their own stories, perhaps, and about Haggard and Mercurius. All right God, summoned or not, You are here. Where are You?

I feel myself sitting in that forest and it is rich and green. I think of the forest of W.H. Hudson and *Green Mansions* and his heroine. Now I think of my wife, having the same name, and her face, smiling at me from behind a tree. Her joy of life, her love, her humor, all make me smile, just to see her here. As I smile, my depression lifts, but I hold my head in my hands, thinking of my many failures.

"Oh Angel of God," I call out. "I am no longer a Knight, no longer a hero of any kind, whether son or grandson. I am but a man who has struggled hard, has been, like Jacob, injured in thigh and mouth and heart in his encounter with you, Angel of God. But I am but a man. I, like Jung, embrace Philemon and sacrifice Faust. I embrace my smallness, devotion, humanness, and give up my expansive and power-seeking efforts to contain all of You, even though You want it. I sit here speechless and unknown. Here I am."

"And here am I" come the words, and I think the Angel is present. But I mistrust. God is always here, I know. But I mistrust the quickness of response. I mistrust the face it presents to me because so many faces and responses have come, yet there has been so much illusion.

"I know your face, Angel, I know your face, Mercurius. Trickster are you as well as Comforter. But lead me to the Higher God, lead me to Him and Her who can truly comfort me. Give me peace. Let the many parts of me come together in harmony. I have been devoted and true, respect the Goddess, been a pilgrim of the Self. So, Angel of God, come and speak."

I see a face, but it is my own face, just as it is now, as I approach my fiftieth year. It is I: greying, lined, serious, with intense eyes, yet capable of laughter. I am an angel of God. I am a representative on earth of the Most High. I go to and fro and search men's hearts. I am a bringer of good things and tell of the Lord. And I, too, am a dark Angel who suffers the torments of hell. I have caused others pain, it is true, and myself as well. The pain I have caused has been unintentional, for the most part, and from a place where my Self does not match the Self of the other, in love or in spirit. My own agony has been of the Lord, in defeat and fragmentation. So then, I am an Angel, light and dark. As an Angel, I have fulfilled my task, Lord. I am your Angel, here on earth, even holding those painful remains of "wings" lost. My shoulder blades ache, and here I am, wingless.

So, I, an Angel, sit here in the forest on a stump. Quiet. Alone. No words come from God, and my own become silenced. Yet I feel calmer, less depressed. I know who I am. I am an Angel, a fragment of God, come to roost on this earth. And my fellow creatures are angels, too, thoughts of God. But many do not know it. They do not know the heaven and hell of it. When I have told of it in my stories, some hear, some do not. Few know that they are angels. I would rise from my torment, Oh Lord, and be a happy angel of God.

Having said that, I see myself rising, along with the tree stump, high into the sky, up to heaven. Feeling the warmth of the sun, I rise up high to the Throne of God, wherein sits that old King upon the highest perch. There, too, as I look, I see that it is I who sits upon that Throne. I am the God up to whom I come. I look into that face, sitting there, quiet and meditative, yet looking at me. It is I. Just as Jung who rose when old and saw that it was he, himself, who dreamed himself. And, I think: well, Jung has had this experience, and so have I. But there is something not right about it. Am I merely inflated? To think that I am an Angel and am God? I understand that the Angel is a representative of God, being both high and low, emissary and inspired one as well as a creature suffering the hell of God, too. But to be God? Perhaps, as Jung was, to know that one is also one's higher Self and living it. It is this Self, to be sure, who unites all that I am. But having said that, having known that, then what?

What it is, is that the ordinary man, the no.1 as Jung called him, can talk to the "Great Man" within, the number 2 who is also the one who combines all the parts. My paradox, though, is that the poor fellow sitting here, he who aches, is depressed and in pain, is also the number 2, the one who can be an angel and do all those things. The paradox is true, but also only partial. It is true that I am those things. But what about that higher God who is greater than my wholeness? Where is He who has arranged all these things?

Now my neck aches, for I am reduced back into myself. There is no Allah but Allah and there is no Marvin but Marvin! So I laugh. But where is the Marvin who can redeem me, the unknowing, paining, disillusioned Marvin? Where is he? That fellow who sits, in fantasy, upon his throne in the sky? ... I see him there, now, laughing at me, with me. And now, the inner world seems silly, too. I am merely stuck with myself, high and low. O.K. Stop writing, start walking.

... I come back from my walk and I am with the "not-I", in response to the "I", as paradoxical as it is. And this leads to writing about the Jungian archetype, but not here.

OCTOBER 6, 1975

It is six days later, and I am in a similar place to that which I wrote about before. In between, it is true, I had moments, hours even, of great joy, of feeling that I was close to wholeness, to ending my "failure" books, and that soon all would be well. I had achieved a certain freedom from the publisher, had been able to distribute books to bookstores myself, had recovered from my paralysis at his hands, and had hopes for new publishers or distributors. I had also done much better in other parts of my life. But this paled in time and, since yesterday, I have felt similar to a week ago. Is this the rhythm of my life, my month, my week? Is this the flow, high and low? Perhaps.

But I have re-read what I wrote six days ago, and it seems decent writing to me, though hardly in a condition to be "printed" — not because of style, grammar, or content, but because of the confusion between the One and the Many of my roles, figures, states. How can this be written or resolved? By a Magician? By the mere honesty of saying it all?

I return to the forest, the place of Tewfik, this land where the stream runs. I sit on the stump of the demolished tree and smile. Many trees are all about. I can even recall "The Tree" — tree. But what, pray tell, does the Self beyond or in all of this want?

"Self, You to whom I prayed a week ago, You who are the uniter of all that I am and all that goes beyond me as well, You, pray, make yourself known to me" ... No answer. There is a leaf, dead and fallen. Another falls. And yet another. The wind blows gently. Is it fall? Is it in the stillness itself? Is stillness the answer? ... No, the stillness precedes. The stillness is the fulsome container. I sense a kind of fountain in the fullness, a semi-material subtle body which emerges out of nothing. It is like sheets or folded cassocks, material which is at once writing paper for a writer, sheets for a healer, cassocks for a priest. A teacher rises out of it and is their combination. It is emptiness and fullness, stillness and words. Out of this sheaf of subtle body material arises which teaches. It teaches me and, through me, others. I look at this ...

As I write this, a local Jungian analyst telephones. He wants to work with me. He has read my book, loved it, feels that only I and my friend B are creative in the Jungian area. So, the teacher symbol reaches out. Let me stay with it.

It looks like a stack of wheat, fasces it is called, but the material is of a subtle body, able to take on the quality of a sheet for a bed or couch, the canvas of a monk or priest, the white typing paper for a writer. And the Teacher, a vapor actually, comes out of it. It is three dimensional, earthy, the product of long labors, produced in the autumn of life (falling leaves, stillness of the moment), and yet spiritual. This is the Self, the harvest of the years of work. I am almost fifty, beginning the Autumn of my life. If each month is six years of our biblical three-score and ten, then I have passed eight months and am one-third of the way through the ninth month. That is to say, about the tenth of September. And this is what comes then. Autumn, and the Self is a Fasces-Sheaf. The Fasces of writer, priest, healer, out of which comes teacher. Gathered, ready for nourishment. Ready to be bread unto others. All right, Self. I accept.

# THE UNPUBLISHED WRITER: EPILOGUE
## (1996)

So ends the tale of the Unpublished Writer. The sympathetic reader will be glad to know that not only did he (I) manage to sell the remaining copies of his book, *The Tree: Tales in Psycho-Mythology,* himself, but that, after a suitable purgation of almost seven years, he did indeed find a new publisher! This new organization, Falcon Press (now New Falcon Publications), was under the guidance of Christopher S. Hyatt, Ph.D., who did indeed understand what my projects were about.

In 1982, I wrote a book called *Buddhism and Jungian Psychology,* co-authored with my friend and colleague, Rev. Mokusen Miyuki, Ph.D. Since that time, I have co-authored and edited a whole series in the area of Jungian psychology and religion, including works on Buddhism; Judaism; Hinduism; Catholicism; Sufism and Islam; and Protestantism, respectively. In addition to that — and more germane to my fellow suffering writers of fiction (I was always able to publish my professional articles without much difficulty) — Falcon Press not only brought out *The Tree* once more, but also, in due course, published its two sequels, *The Quest* and *The Love,* the latter's title suitably changed to *Jungian Psychology and the Passions of the Soul,* since it was less a work of pure fiction than that of mythology with psychological commentary. Other works, on therapy, for example, have also been published. I am glad to say that all have done well and that some of the books have already undergone second and third printings.

I do not mean to brag about all this but rather to say: "Take heart, fellow unpublished writers, it can happen after all!" In my case, the "promise" of Muse and divine representative turned out to be fulfilled, although heavily delayed. The fact is that this book *The Unpublished Writer* only appears some four years after its sister book *The Unhealed Healer,* but it does appear! Since then I have indeed continued a long series on "Failures and Successes." Briefly, the "real" figures of Healer and Writer join an Unfrocked Priest, an Empty Teacher, a Powerless Magician — all failures — along with the Tewfik Lady, a Scholar Baroness, and Maya the Yogini, in a several-volumed group process, transforming failure into success. These, too, I trust, will ultimately find "embodiment" as books.

One might speculate that the whole point and purpose of the suffering was to be able to write these books, perhaps, and speak for that unhappy group of writers and of healers whose pain in their craft and vocation cry out for expression. The reader might be interested in what Henry Miller once told me, when I cautiously asked him if he could prod a publisher to seriously consider my work. He told me the story of the boy who had watched a struggling chrysalis. The lad tried to "help" by assisting it to get out; result: dead chrysalis, no butterfly. If Miller's intuition was correct — about me, at least — *this* butterfly was meant to suffer, precisely in order to produce the present book. Who knows about others? In any case, I am glad to report that my own myth continues to unfold and I wish God's speed and fulfillment to all those who are pursuing their own!

# APPENDIX

*The Unpublished Writer: Part II of 30-plus Year Report to*
*Alma Mater*                                    *(Spring 1991)*

(Note: The following is the second of two lectures delivered by
the author to students and faculty at the C.G. Jung Institute
Zürich on the occasion of his return there for a visit in the spring
of 1991, having earned the Analyst's Diploma in 1959. The first
lecture, "The Unhealed Healer", can be found in the companion
book to this series, entitled *Reich, Jung, Regardie & Me: The
Unhealed Healer*.)

In my previous lecture, I spoke at length about my development as an analyst, beginning with that prescient dream which I
had at the end of my training in Zürich in early 1959, leading up
to the present. I shall now do something similar with my development as a writer, beginning once more with the part of that
same dream which took place immediately after my wrestle with
the analyst. You will recall that after I left both analyst and
Institute secretary, I was confronted by my maternal grandmother
who pointed, auspiciously, to an intense, wild-eyed figure in a
bricked-in room, open only at the roof to a star-filled sky in the
midst of a regular sun-shiny one. That man wrote furiously,
stopping periodically as if to address an unseen presence, presumably divine. At the time, I interpreted this figure as a representation of my own intense work with active imagination and
understood it to mean that this activity would continue for me, as
it did, upon my return to California. This was surely a correct
interpretation — at least for the next seven-plus years — as I
relied upon this tried-and-true method of Jung to keep my
connection with the unconscious and provide a water of life in
the — to me — parched desert of my native soil.

Just after Christmas of 1966, however, almost eight years later, I was in my office, reflecting on the previous year's events. In the spring, feeling unjustly treated, I had resigned from my local analytic society. I had been professionally rather alone, therefore, but really enjoying it. For some six months, I had been working on a fantasy which took place in a cave and involved a mother and daughter, a man of ancient age and a young boy who did not speak. As I continued with this active imagination, there suddenly appeared a Knight, dressed in black with a golden sun emblazoned on his chest. The Knight took the mother and daughter on his horse and ran off. Startled, I pursued this figure, recognizing him from a dream I had shortly after my resignation. In that dream, I was on a field of battle, perhaps in Macedonia. The Knight was strong, but battle-scarred and weary. As he smiled at me wanly, I realized that he and I had been engaged in the service of Jungian psychology in the outer world, and now that was going to end. I felt saddened but relieved by the dream in that my decision to resign seemed to be confirmed by the unconscious.

Now, many months later, this Knight was returning. Not only was he back, but he was carrying off my friends. When I caught up with him, I asked him why he did that and he replied that he was trying to get my attention. He certainly had it now, I told him, and he then presented a surprising proposal. He said that he, and also some others in his world, had stories to tell. Would I join them in writing these tales? I was not to be a mere amanuensis, just take dictation, but was expected to participate and contribute my own reactions and reflections as well. These stories, furthermore, were not only for my own edification and enjoyment, but were intended for a larger public.

Although I was startled by this proposition from the Knight, I was also excited by it. I had written stories in my adolescence, and even when I was a child, a favorite aunt had taken down an attempted tale of mine. For a time, in my teens, having written for school publications, I thought to become a journalist and even wrote a book about my experiences as a sailor in the Merchant Marine during World War II. I had doubts about my skill as a writer, however. When I completed my sailor's book at age twenty, I hoped that, if it were published, I would go back to sea, write travel and short stories until I was forty, at which time I might be mature enough to write novels. When the book was not accepted for publication, I realized that I had to find some other career and gradually decided on psychology. So, here I was now, many years later, in 1966, faced with the prospect of writing once more. But now I was, indeed, the very age of forty that I had magically selected for such work when I was twenty!

Not only did the story-writing of my youth return, but I also remembered two other occasions in which this Knight-theme appeared powerfully in my life. The first time was when I was less than four years old, just before my family moved from east Lost Angeles to the southwest part of the city. I had been seated on my little tricycle on the sidewalk in front of my parent's house. I remembered awaking from a deep dream or fantasy, and not knowing what it was that I dreamed or imagined, but feeling its impact. Then I felt the power of the sun directly above me. In the way that a child of less than four can understand such things, I felt that the sun was connected with God. But then I had the feeling that such a golden sun was also at my chest, inside. I was bemused by there being a sun above in the sky and a sun within me. I was also struck by the words "sun" and "son" and felt myself to be, somehow, a son of the sun. I felt quite special and very competent on my little tricycle, able to steer it quite well.

In the midst of this sense of power and well-being, however, I looked back at the house and felt my mother's presence there. As light and warm were the sun, as dark and uncertain were the house and my mother. Next door lived two little girls, one of whom was my friend, but the other one had scratched me. She, too, was dark and uncertain. There I was, faced with the problem of the opposites of sun and moon, light and dark, masculine and feminine, the three (tricycle) and two (mother and little girl). Not that I understood anything of this at that age, of course, but I now realized, at age forty, that the Knight made his first appearance then. He also made me aware of the opposites, with my poor mother and the little girl as ripe objects for my projections. I had to wait for mid-life, however, to find out what this Knight was all about.

The second appearance of the Knight — or his representatives — occurred twenty-one years later, when I was twenty-five. It was the summer of 1951 and I was a living a kind of hermit's life. I had completed my job as a teaching assistant in the psychology department of the UCLA graduate school and was preparing to start my internship with the Veteran's Administration hospitals and clinics. I had also temporarily taken some weeks off from my Jungian analysis and was happily spending my time totally alone, except for my dog, in my little one-room house over a garage near the university. After several rather prescient dreams, I one night dreamed as follows:

> I am traveling around the world as a sailor with Marco Polo when suddenly a whirlwind comes up and envelops me. It thrusts me into the Underworld where I meet the poet Virgil, who now accompanies me on adventures. The most significant of these is an encounter with a large green dragon who spits red and yellow fire. I battle this dragon and overcome it. Exhausted, I find myself alone on a kind of medieval street, but now, rather than in brilliant color, the dream continues in greys, black and white. I wander, weakened and alone, when suddenly a door opens up. Two huge Knights, dressed in green with golden suns on their chests, grab me and bring me inside to a large circular arena, brilliantly lighted and in intense color. The two Knights then proceed to beat me with branches from a tree, but as in a ritual, not with violence. After the beating, I see a crowd of people, among whom are a handsome French couple and my professor and employer, Dr. Bruno Klopfer. They all look expectantly at me and then all eyes turn towards a huge crown, shimmering with diamonds and other precious stones. The crown is of great beauty and majesty and I am enthralled by it, until I realize that I am about to be crowned. I see that this crown is far too large for me and I take a step back, overwhelmed with the prospect. As I retreat, the pleasure and anticipation of the crowd turns to sorrow. I hear them say, in alternating sentences, as if undecided, "he is unworthy" or "he is too young." I awaken sobbing and with the realization that there are levels of the psyche far deeper than anything I had yet encountered.

When I had written down this powerful dream, I remembered the event of my early childhood, but the true significance of all this had to await the reappearance of the Knight, in both dream and fantasy, when I was forty. Suffice it to say that this hero myth faced me at ages four and twenty-five, but I was only ready to take it on consciously at the age of forty. The Crown of the Self, of course, was too big for me earlier on and, in some ways, it is too big for me even now. The personal part of the Self can certainly be carried by me, but I discovered that the archetypal Self, as symbolized by the Crown, is to be found as the highest Sephira in Kabbalah in Jewish mysticism and also represents the highest chakra in Kundalini Yoga of Hinduism. As such, it refers to the SELF, the God of us all, that Christmas Humphreys is talking about when he contrasts the self (ego) with the Self (personal inner authority) and the SELF (transcendent, inclusive totality).

It is also not by chance that this Crown symbolism, so important in Kabbalah, should appear in the dream. My very first active imagination, at age twenty-five, did not contain a crown but connected me quite shakingly with the *Zohar,* that central text in Jewish Kabbalistic mysticism, in a starling way. I had completed a written fantasy, along with some paintings, all of which I called, "Purple in the Blue." When I came to the waiting room of my first analyst, Dr. Max Zeller, I found there, resting on the table, the five volumes of the *Zohar,* in English translation. They had just arrived. I picked up a volume at random and opened it somewhere in the middle. To my astonishment, I read therein a fantasy which was remarkably similar to the one I had just written! I walked up to Dr. Zeller's office, trembling with this experience of synchronicity. So one can see that the level from which the Knight came was indeed most powerful and deep.

To return now to my conversation with the Knight after Christmas 1966, more than fifteen years later: I was reminded of all that happened before in connection with this figure and was now faced with the possibility of continuing my relation with him, but in a more conscious and equal fashion. I therefore consented to the writing work with the Knight and his friends, provided that this could be limited to two days per week. After all, I had a wife, children, and an analytic practice. Luckily, I had just ended a seven-year teaching position at UCLA. So, then, my story-writing began.

The Knight's tale proved to be a gnostic encounter with the image of God as in a fragmented condition, requiring human connection to bring about wholeness. It was indeed Kabbalistic and Christian and Pagan and brought an experience of meaningful connection among several myths: Biblical genesis, Christian incarnation, the Greek feminine and creativity, and gnostic integration. The tale made use of much of the symbolism that I experienced in my "big" dream plus more than I could have anticipated. If nothing else, this story-writing made the autonomy of the unconscious abundantly clear!

The Knight's tale was followed by that of an Arab whose theme was the struggle with passion and love. The tale drew somewhat on my experience as a Merchant Marine traveling the world during World War II, particularly in Egypt and India, but the theme was expressed in the context of Muslim piety. One result was a mandala with a crescent moon and star.

The third tale was that of a Japanese Ronin, a samurai without a lord, whose adventures and enlightenment were in close conjunction with the images and poems of that strikingly impactful series of drawings and poems, the Ox-Herding Pictures of Zen Buddhism. All three of these stories were clearly based on the hero myth, but each man experienced this in connection with the individuation process.

Following the three heroes, there appeared several women, in sequence. Indeed, the remainder of the tales of women — five in number and equal to those of the men — constituted stages in what Jung referred to as the development of the feminine in a man, the *anima*. The first woman's story was that of "Julia, the Atheist-Communist," who struggled with the problem of coming to be a mother on the one hand and with her atheism, on the other. The second woman's story was "Sybilla, the Nymphomaniac." Hers, a Pagan tale, was the transformation of prostitute into prophetess and the bride of God. "Maria, the Nun" was the third tale, one of a modern Catholic woman's engagement with the images of God.

After the three women's tales, those of men resumed, alternating with the remaining women. First was that of "The African," which was a story of an American black man finding his spiritual roots in an alchemical work with an Abyssinian woman. This was followed by the story of "Maya, the Yogini," a Hindu woman who pursued Kundalini Yoga in what one might now call a feminist fashion. Then came the story of an "Old Chinese Man" who had an ongoing dialogue with his dreams, Taoism, and the *I Ching*. Finally, there was the tale of "The Medium," Sophie-Sarah, who addressed the horrors of the Holocaust, using Kabbalistic knowledge. There were ten stories in all, along with poems by each seeker. The tales and persons represented ten different religions, attitudes or belief-systems, but all were individuation stories. They met at the Tree of Life in Paradise, and all found their own symbols fruitfully growing thereon. That book, therefore, was called, *The Tree: Tales in Psycho-Mythology.*

Hardly had I completed that first book, however, when there appeared a young man calling himself the Son of the Knight. He wanted to continue the story-telling in a new book. He, it turned out, was from that original fantasy of the silent boy, old man, mother and daughter, in the cave. His tale proved to be also one of individuation, but now, in contrast to *The Tree,* the stories involved pairs. The first part of the book, for example, was that of the Son of the Knight and his companion, Dog. The second part was that of Mother and Daughter. The Son of the Knight had a hero's quest as part of it, although rather different from the standard one, while the tale of the Mother and Daughter included the Demeter-Persephone theme in the background, but also had Christian aspects to it. The third part of the book shifted from dyads to triads and made use of the story of King Arthur, Queen Guinevere and Sir Lancelot. The whole book rounded out, finally, in a search for the Grail. This second book was called, *The Quest: Further Tales in Psycho-Mythology.*

Not much time elapsed before a third volume began, this one called, *The Love.* As one might expect, the book explored multiple images and forms of love, including Don Juan, Jesus, Aphrodite and the Muses, as well as Eros. It was undertaken by — guess who? — the Grandson of the Knight! The tree symbolism of the first book, developed further in the second, was rounded in the third by an amalgamation of Kundalini Yoga, Magic, Kabbalah, and other symbols by means of stories, historical reconstructions and meditations.

The entire trilogy, about two thousand typewritten pages in length, took approximately four years to complete. Confident of what the Knight had told me in the first place — that the work was meant not just for me but for a larger public, and also buoyed up by the positive response to it from my friend, the author Henry Miller, and the support of Anais Nin, I sent the first book out to various publishers. After several years and forty rejections, I thought there might be some mistake — either in the Knight's predictive capacity, his assessment of my skill or in the receptivity of the times.

At last, however, a small publisher was found for *The Tree.* This publisher, alas, went bankrupt — not, I hasten to add, because of my book, since the thousand printed copies did sell out. At that point, I resumed my writing, but the title of my next work became *The Failures.* The heroes of that work, if one can call them that, were an Unpublished Writer, an Unhealed Healer, an Empty Teacher and an Unfrocked Priest! They all met, at last, at the mountain retreat of the Powerless Magician. That book almost ended in failure, of course, but after a time, there was a sequel to it, called *The Successes,* in which that same group of people continued their exploration to fulfillment.

In the meantime, another publisher appeared. He reprinted *The Tree* in 1982, published *The Quest* in 1984, and brought out *The Love,* now retitled, *Jungian Psychology and the Passions of the Soul* — since it was, indeed, no longer an exclusively fictional work — in 1989.

This same publisher has also been interested in my nonfictional work, so that, in the last nine years, he has published books I have written and edited on the relation of Jungian psychology to the various religions (Buddhism, Judaism, Hinduism, Catholicism, Islam and Protestantism) as well as a book on analysis and other works. As I mentioned earlier, two books I wrote in the early 1970's, called *The Unhealed Healer* and *The Unpublished Writer,* will also appear soon. The former is an account of my Reichian therapy and the latter goes over the ground of those same years of unrequited passion for publication, alone on a magical journey with the deceased writer, H. Rider Haggard. So, the frustrated failure can now happily enjoy a degree of success. Indeed, after certain others of my books get finished, I plan to complete that one, too.

So, that is the story of my stories. What does it all mean? Is it a kind of hero or anti-hero myth of myself? Yes, I think so, but I think that there is more to it and I wish to address myself to what it might mean beyond that.

Jung, you will recall, made a strict distinction between active imagination and art. The former was aimed at the creation of the personality rather than towards works of art. One must clearly find a balance between the need for understanding and the aesthetic need in such a psychological endeavor, he asserted. In his *Memoirs,* Jung tells us how he was tempted by a siren feminine voice, both inner and outer, who told him that his work was "art." He manfully resisted that insinuation and persuaded himself — and us, I think — that his work was in the interest of science. What was needed was for the person to understand and transform himself, not just be a mouthpiece for the unconscious which, perhaps, some artists become.

That Jung took this tack is certainly a good thing for the rest of us. Many of his discoveries came from this work. Nor does his writing — for instance, the *Sermones ad Mortuos* — seem particularly artistic, although some of his paintings are quite impressive. This is the case with most products of active imagination, as we know. They may have some artistic merit, but they are clearly expressive of the individual psyche rather than works of art which are of interest to others.

How, then, do I view my own story-writing? Is it perhaps failed art or active imagination misunderstood? I think not. First of all, I did regular active imagination for sixteen years before even beginning that kind of story-writing. Secondly, the material which appears, as I have said, is in the form of tales told by figures from the unconscious. If it is active imagination, it is done by the archetypal figures themselves. This, I think, brings it beyond the personal level to a transpersonal one. Thirdly, whether or not it is art remains to be determined by time and criticism. The stories and books need to walk about on their own legs and see if they can manage in the literary world and effect people. They have had some impact so far, but we shall see to what extent this continues.

I originally described this kind of work, wherein a Jungian analyst was writing mythological stories, as a new genre, "psycho-mythology." I hope that this was not an inflationary neologism. It just seemed to me that a form of art was in the making, something like science-fiction or the historical novel. In the latter two genres, there is an amalgamation of imagination with either scientific facts and theories or with historical knowledge. In psycho-mythology, I thought, there was a union, in story form, between psychological knowledge and imagination.

There has been other psychological fiction, of course, but has there been fiction influenced by Jung's discoveries, or that which would touch on the mythological level of the psyche? Not to my knowledge. In the years from 1967 to the '70's, when I was so

engaged, there was not the interest in Jung that there is now and
there were no colleagues of mine so occupied. Someone has
called my attention to the writing of Ursula Le Guin, a science-
fiction writer, who has written knowledgeably about Jung (in
*Language of the Night,* 1979). I have not yet read her fictional
work, so I can not tell, but one does not yet know whether there
is a new genre or not, or even the extent to which Jung's work
will have an effect on the literary/artistic mind.

I have to ask myself, however, how I understand the writing I
have done psychologically? That it is clearly part of my own
myth and individuation process goes without saying. One might
even claim, with fairness, that the work *is* my myth. I would not
quarrel with this conclusion, but I would add that parts of my
myth are not included in it, that other myths are, and that the
myth is continuing. I would also agree that the contents can be
interpreted. In much of the writing, however, the psychological
view-point, as well as interpretation, is embedded in it. I would
even go so far as to say that part of the claim that this a new
genre lies in the fact that interpretation is part of the work itself,
is in the service of the story-telling. Some psychological criticism and interpretation of artistic work tends to be reductive and
even destructive. The critic stands apart and comments or fires
barbs at the creative person as well as the work. With psycho-
mythology, however, interpretation does not stand outside and
apart, but is part of the art itself and serves it. If interpretation is
not part of the art or does not advance the process, it is largely
useless, if not destructive. This is one form of psychological
understanding of psycho-mythology.

Another way to understand what I am doing in such writing, I
found in that branch of Jewish mysticism and magic called
Kabbalah. It comes from the central image therein, the Tree of
Life. That Tree, you will recall, encompasses ten-fold aspects of
the divine, just as the Trinity encompasses three-fold aspects. In
the center of the Tree, half-way up — for those who "climb" the
Tree for their apprehension and relationship with God — is the
sephira (as it is called)) of Tiphereth. This is the androgynous
God-man-woman position on the Tree, and also that of beauty
and art. The seeker comes up from his mortal existence to it. One
could just as easily say "down," since the Tree of Life has its
roots in heaven and grows down in polarities towards us.

At Tiphereth, one experiences a union of the divine and the human. I would say that each of the hero-figures of my fictional books is divine and mortal or, seen psychologically, is archetypal and personal. I myself climb up to them and when they, in turn, are having experiences, they are in touch with higher or deeper qualities of the divine principle itself, which I experience along with them. This, it seems to me, is an imaginal representation of Jungian psychology itself. In analytical psychology, we are constantly apprehending the archetypal, but we come to it via our personal experience or with people with whom we work. The claim of psycho-mythology is that the archetypal transcends the personal in this kind of writing, and it may be therefore of more general interest or value. This was the view of the Knight, his friends and heirs, and this is my view too.

One curious thing which has grown out of this writing — and unexpected — has been how these two disparate tracks of my career, healer and writer, have somehow interpenetrated each other in more recent years. For example the last book of the trilogy, beginning with *The Tree* and ending with *The Love*, completed over twenty years ago, has proved to be a cornerstone of my understanding of my most recent work in therapy. The system resulting in that book, combining Kundalini, Kabbalah, Jungian psychology, magic and mythology, has really been a basis for the psychological energy work I now do with some analysands. The "mutual process" procedure I have followed all these years has been underpinned by a theory of centers and energy which has drawn on all of my work, including Reichian therapy. Even active imagination, which was the origin of my writing, has continued to be of central importance in therapy, but now also appears as a kind of joint active imagination in the therapeutic process.

In a way, this should be no surprise, really, since all of this has surely been a story of my own individuation process, but I am amazed at how islands of development, seemingly far apart, gradually find their common root or direction after years of going their separate ways. When I finally get around to finishing my *Successes* book, perhaps I will see the connections among the writer, healer, teacher and priest as well. Since I will be writing about the root metaphor of each "calling," perhaps their connection with that central symbol of the "tree" will emerge. In a sense, that was already shown in my initial two "failure" books, *The Unhealed Healer* and *The Unpublished Writer.* Both of them, finally, were concerned with the issue of relationship between inner world and outer world, between psychic reality and consensus reality. That work has continued over the years and I understand this naturally as a continuation of the alchemical process, within myself and with my patients, as it has progressed over the years. That the *unus mundus* phase of it all should preoccupy me during the last years will be readily understandable to all who hear this lecture.

Finally, I want to complete this story of my stories by taking up some questions which have emerged when I previously lectured on psycho-mythology. Some of these follow:

QUESTION: Don't you think it is inflated to use such a word as "psycho-mythology"? After all, you are just writing stories and Barbara Hannah, in her book on active imagination, uses the example of story-writing as a pre-cursor to real use of the technique.

ANSWER: There are two questions here. First, I hope it is not inflated to use the term, "psycho-mythology," although it may be a bit pompous. I only intended to delineate an area of new writing and investigation. This area is to be designated as one requiring psychological knowledge and experience which can only come, I believe, from intensive personal analytical work. It also requires whatever one expects from art and is, and should be, subject to the same criticism.

QUESTION: You say your work should be subject to the usual canons of artistic criticism, yet the work was rejected by many publishers and you yourself were in doubt as to your artistic skill.

ANSWER: I agree with you, but who are we to question the positive judgments of Henry Miller, Anais Nin and Gilbert Phelps, Fellow of the Royal Society of Literature in England? All of them thought the work quite worthwhile. Luckily, there is now a publisher who agrees with them and we shall see if these four, plus the Knight, are wrong.

QUESTION: Could you teach other people to do this sort of writing?

ANSWER: No, I don't think so, at least not directly. One would first have to do a lot of active imagination, I think, for its own sake, or the sake of the individuation process. If story-writing came out of that, as it did with me, then the process would go on by itself. What can be taught, however, is the method of active imagination itself, which leads to increased self-understanding, integration, and creativity.

QUESTION: Why do you think that active imagination is not as popular with analysts and patients as it was when Jung was alive?

ANSWER: I do not know. Perhaps because it may lead people "away" from many earthly concerns into the unconscious, and maybe because it is just too hard for many people, particularly in a highly extraverted society. I only know that it has been a great blessing for me.

QUESTION: You say that your kind of writing is new. Has there not been psychological writing that also reaches the level of myth and the collective psyche? Does not all great art, for example, do such a thing?

ANSWER: All great art certainly touches the collective unconscious and springs from there or it would not have its universal appeal. Most art, however, does not have two things characteristic of psycho-mythology, namely the mythic, fantasy aspect and the criterion of being psychologically informed. The latter is the case only because Jung had not yet lived! Let us see how this knowledge and experience effects future generations of writers and artists. I can think, however, of at least one contemporary great work of literature which is similar to psycho-mythology, lacking only a clear indication of being informed by psychological understanding of the Jungian sort. That is the late work of Thomas Mann, *The Holy Sinner.*

QUESTION: I would like to return, if we may, to the contents of your writing. I notice that in your work, the hero, as exemplified by the Knight, becomes the leader or guide and the teller of the tale. In Jung's work, when he parted from Freud, he found it necessary to kill the hero, as he tells us in his dreams about Siegfried. How do you account for this difference?

ANSWER: An interesting question. Somewhere about the age of forty, there is for many people, a shift in attitude, a new relation to the unconscious. The hero archetype is one that is central in this. The hero, for the boy, adolescent and youth, is the central image which leads to the building up of the ego and its capacity to make its way in life. For the man of middle age, the hero must then be overcome — as it was with Jung — because it stands in the way of a new relationship to the unconscious, one of surrender to a new center, the Self, rather than battling the dragons. In my case, the hero did not need to be overcome at middle life, since I was not so identified with him at that time and he performed a further function of relationship to the Self in a creative way, rather than turn me outward toward further conquest or achievement in the world. Jung, I believe, needed to overcome the hero in order to approach the anima and other archetypal figures. Since I had already spent many years in relationship with the anima and other figures of the unconscious, thanks to his techniques of dream analysis and active imagination, I think that the hero image did not stand in the way.

QUESTION: I have another question about the content of your stories. Do you think that some of that material, with its figures from the past and other cultures, could have originated from past lives? In other words, could they have arisen as a result of reincarnational experiences?

ANSWER: I can not answer that in any convincing manner. It is true that sometimes in my writing I have felt that I have known or experienced certain events before. I could not have known some of these things from my own memories in this life. Yet one can not prove that at all. For instance, when I was writing the story of *Maya, the Yogini,* and realized that at one phase she was connected to what is called the *Akasha* center, that hypothesized region wherein one can know one's past lives and other transcendental truths, I felt strongly that I could, indeed, read my own and other people's incarnations. Yet it is also a fact that this kind of connection with some aspects of the unconscious always produces just this kind of experience or belief. It is certainly psychologically true, for that is the way how the unconscious works in that condition. But that is far from proving that such a belief points to a literal truth. For the most part, I really do not care very much, since it is enough for me to have the psychological truth, but I can see that one could investigate such experiences and check them out in an experimental way.

QUESTION: Is the Knight or other of your figures still "alive" in your psyche; that is, is he still a guide or presence?

ANSWER: Not really. He is a fond memory. Sometimes he can be fleshed out with a contemporary and present life, but this life is drawn, I think, from present energy and from memories. I therefore think — and this continues my response to the previous question — that most of what I have written is drawn from an archetypal layer rather than from reincarnational memories. The archetypes, as we know, exist as potentials, as structures, and are filled-in by personal material. They change, therefore, as a person grows and develops. The Knight seems to have accomplished what he had in mind when he first appeared when I was less than four years old and at twenty-five and to have come fully into his own when I reached forty. Since then, he seems to have quietly faded into the background of the psyche as a whole. But who can tell, he may re-emerge with full force and other tasks or questions at any time. The unconscious, after all, is really autonomous and larger than consciousness, so we can not conclusively state anything about its permanent condition, about where it comes from or where it is going. One can only give one's best estimate at the time.

QUESTION: May I return to the topic of active imagination itself? I often feel blocked and self-conscious when I attempt active imagination. What can I do about it?

ANSWER: That is a common response of people at the beginning. They feel that they are "making it up," it is not the real thing. This shows us that in *that* condition we suffer the conscious cramp that western man is heir to and that Jung has written about. We have lost connection with the child-like relation to fantasy which is spontaneous and creative. What Jung did was to follow the imaginative impulses that came up, play with stones, for example. He did little sand-plays with rivulets all of his life. So one way is to do what he did: listen to that playful child's voice or mood and do what it wants, lovingly but consciously, until one begins to feel the reality of the soul once more.

Another way is to talk to the block itself. Let that wall of resistance speak. That reminds me of another time, early in my first analysis. I had been going along for several months, fascinated with the process of working with fantasy, dreams and active imagination, when suddenly it all stopped. Nothing. It felt like a stone or brick wall. My analyst, Dr. Zeller, said, why not let the wall speak? I thought, all right, my mother used to say, when I was an adolescent, that sometimes talking to me was like talking to a wall, so I can try to do what he says. I then gave lips to that wall of resistance in my fantasy and waited for it to speak. When it did, I had a shock. What it said remains with me even now, forty years later, and it took me quite a while to fully understand what it was all about. Here is some of what the wall said:

Where in the thunder of the Name is the ghost?
Look for it there behind the Tree.
Go back to the place where you found the worm.
Holy man, hollow man;
Solo-man, Solomon.

That voice came powerfully like an Old Testament prophet or like God Himself. Rather than interpret it now — it took me a long time to sort it out, as I have said — I would rather tell you that the particular kind of energy in the voice is one that I felt, some years ago, when I stood before the Western Wall, the Wall of Lamentation, in Jerusalem. The heat and energy coming out of the wall shook me; it spoke to me in just the same way as the wall of fantasy did so many years ago. At the time of my initial experience, when I was twenty-five years old, my analyst commented that the unconscious was indeed layered and structured like a wall, and that this particular wall was like a voice from God. It was a full and clear representation of the reality of the Self for me, far beyond my own powers to control or direct. I can't say that all deep resistances are like that, of course, but I do recommend that one honor such a wall and permit it to speak.

QUESTION: I notice that the tree image also appears in this conversation — exhortation, really — from the wall. Your fictional books have tree symbolism as central, it seems. Did you have other dreams or visions with this theme?

ANSWER: Oh yes, many! That's why it was so important a symbol for me. I mentioned the theme of the Knights beating me with branches from a tree. Another important dream, towards the end of my Jungian analyses altogether — that is, after about eight years of work — I dreamed that I was standing at a podium, about to give a lecture, when a large trunk of a tree, filled with powerful energy, perhaps even explosive, was handed to me. Many people had been handed this tree trunk, it seems, but no one wanted to risk holding it. But somebody had to do it, so I accepted the trunk and bowed my head, surrendering to God's will. Some months later, when I went back to Zürich for analysis there, I felt the need to do a series of paintings, which ended up with a — to me — impressive flowering tree, both containing and becoming a mandala. I knew then that I no longer was in need of an analyst on the outside. The Self was solidly within.

It was four years after that event that my writing the book, *The Tree*, began. Of course, each of these dreams and events triggers other memories and dreams which could be related. I would rather say, however, that the psyche itself is like a tree, with many leaves and flowers and fruit, continually unfolding, reaching up into heaven and down into the depths of the earth. It is a good image for the growth and expression of the Self. The many dreams, the writing and the events are all manifestations of the unfolding of that Self image for me and my honoring it.

QUESTION: You spoke of cooperative work and change of personality. Could you say that the Knight and the other characters changed too?

ANSWER: Yes, we both developed. In a sense, I really don't know how much was me, how much the Knight. There was mutual change: blurring, differentiation, integration. In the end, I think, as I have said, the content which belonged to me, in contrast to the archetype itself, has been integrated and expressed, and now I have moved on. I would have to ask the Knight his opinion about that, though.

QUESTION: After you started writing, how did your life change?

ANSWER: Everything changed and nothing changed., I remained the same plodding clinician, the same man with family and friends. But I also committed myself as a writer and one who ever since has been in the service of producing and making manifest the creative spirit which presented itself to me. It was, in short, the individuation process, with its own joys, as well as the pains of grief, despair, automatic inflation when one falls away from the collective. With it all, however, has come a sense of fulfillment, particularly since my writing has been published. Finally, it was included with the rest of my life, in my attempt to follow my individual path and still find my place in community life. That process continues.

# PUBLICATIONS IN PSYCHO-MYTHOLOGY

*The Tree: Tales in Psycho-Mythology*, Phoenix House, Los Angeles, 1974. 463 plus ix pp. (reprinted as a paperback by Falcon Press, Phoenix, AZ, 1982 and subsequently reprinted by New Falcon Publications, Tempe, AZ, 1993 under the title *The Tree of Life: Paths in Jungian Individuation*).

*The Knight,* Falcon Press, Phoenix, AZ, 1982, 87 pp.

*The Quest,* Falcon Press, Phoenix, AZ, 1984, 175 plus x pp.

*The Nymphomaniac,* Falcon Press, Phoenix, AZ, 1985, 78 pp.

*Jungian Psychology & the Passions of the Soul* (The Love), Falcon Press, Phoenix, AZ, 1989, 446 plus ix pp.

*Reich, Jung, Regardie & Me: The Unhealed Healer,* New Falcon Publications, Tempe, AZ, 1996.

*Rider Haggard, Henry Miller & I: The Unpublished Writer,* New Falcon Publications, Tempe, AZ, 1997.

# FROM J. MARVIN SPIEGELMAN, PH.D.

## PSYCHOTHERAPY AS A MUTUAL PROCESS

C.G. Jung originated the realization that not only did the analyst need to be analyzed first, but that the therapeutic process ultimately involves the mutual transformation of both participants. J. Marvin Spiegelman has been the foremost advocate and explicator of this view, and his newest book clearly and colorfully describes the evolution of both theory and practice of what is now called "the interactive field."

ISBN 1-56184-063-7

## REICH, JUNG, REGARDIE AND ME

*The Unhealed Healer*

An intimate journey of self discovery. Dr. Spiegelman shares his personal record of more than seven years of Neo-Reichian therapy with the famed mystic/practitioner Dr. Israel Regardie.

"...a courageous book. It reveals what really happens in analysis.
— Dr. med. Adolf Guggenbuhl-Craig, C. G. Jung Institute, Zürich

ISBN 1-56184-032-7

# FROM J. MARVIN SPIEGELMAN, PH.D.

## BUDDHISM AND JUNGIAN PSYCHOLOGY

**With Mokusen Miyuki, Ph.D.**

A masterful description and analysis of mystical states which makes Buddhism meaningful for the Westerner. A breakthrough book and a must for students of the Buddhist tradition. Beautifully illustrated.

"An extraordinary job of unifying the concepts underlying Jungian Psychology and Buddhism.
— Dr. Israel Regardie

ISBN 1-56184-111-0

**Buddhism and Jungian Psychology**

By J. Marvin Spiegelman, Ph.D.
and Mokusen Miyuki, Ph.D.
Buddhist Priest

## CATHOLICISM AND JUNGIAN PSYCHOLOGY

A masterwork of the highest degree, Catholicism and Jungian Psychology is a rare example of a cooperative venture done right. Created by an ecumenical group of twenty-one renowned Jungian analysts, psychologists, and scholars from many religious traditions. Filled with thought-provoking material that is both timely and timeless.

ISBN 1-56184-036-X

**Catholicism and Jungian Psychology**

EDITED BY J. MARVIN SPIEGELMAN, Ph.D.
Contributing Authors:
Magda Arnold, Ph.D. ☐ Sister Noreen Cannon, CSJ, Ph.D.
Gerd Max Cryns, Ph.D. ☐ Rev. Robert M. Doran, Ph.D.
Rev. John P. Dourley, Ph.D. ☐ Rev. John M. Harrington, Ph.D.
Rev. Thomas M. Hedberg, M.A. ☐ Baroness Vera von der Heydt
Rev. Russel Peter Holmes, M.A. ☐ Rev. Thomas Immoos, Ph.D.
Rev. Kevin N. Kerbawy ☐ Thomas F. Lavin, Ph.D. ☐ Terrence McBride
Rev. John P. McHenry, SVD ☐ John Meany, Ph.D. ☐ Rabbi Levi Meier, Ph.D.
Rev. Mokusen Miyuki, Ph.D. ☐ Rev. Roger J. Radloff, Ph.D.
J. Marvin Spiegelman, Ph.D. ☐ Rev. Thomas Stehly, M.A.
Lucia van Ruiten, M.A., BHM

# FROM J. MARVIN SPIEGELMAN, PH.D.

## PROTESTANTISM AND JUNGIAN PSYCHOLOGY

"I strongly advocate a revision of our religious formulas with the aid of psychological insight. It is the great advantage of Protestantism that an intelligent discussion is possible. Protestantism should make use of this freedom." — Carl Gustav Jung

*Protestantism & Jungian Psychology* provides the opportunity for thirteen well-known Protestants and others to heed Jung's call. Among them are Paul Tillich, Hanna Hadorn, Andreas Schweizer-Vullers and Joseph Wagenseller.

ISBN 1-56184-120-X

**Protestantism and Jungian Psychology**

Edited By J. Marvin Spiegelman

Contributing Authors
Michael Anderton • Lars Elmberg
Fred R. Gustafson • Hanna Hadorn
Astri Hognestad • Julia M. Jewett
Thomas Patrick Lavin • Andreas Schweizer-Vullers
J. Marvin Spiegelman • Murray Stein
Weaver Stevens • Paul Tillich
Joseph Wagenseller

## SUFISM, ISLAM AND JUNGIAN PSYCHOLOGY

### With Pir Vilayat Inayat Khan and Tasnim Fernandez

Here is a unique study of Sufism, the ultimate mystical doctrine at the very heart of Islam, analyzed within a Jungian context. With contributions by Pir Vilayat Inayat Khan, the Head of the Sufi Order in the West, and other internationally famous contributors.

ISBN 1-56184-015-7

**Sufism, Islam and Jungian Psychology**

J. Marvin Spiegelman, Ph.D.
with Pir Vilayat Inayat Khan
and Tasnim Fernandez